The Ultimate World Building Book

Characters, Cultures, and More

Casia Schreyer

All rights reserved. © 2018, Casia Schreyer

The author references several television shows, movies, franchises, and books as examples throughout this book. Casia Schreyer and Schreyer Ink Publishing do not claim any ownership of or rights to any of these references.

References made to Casia Schreyer's own works are copyrighted by the author.

ISBN 978-1-988853-18-5

To Stephanie, for building a world with me so many years ago

To Jonathan, for loving me and for supporting me as I chase my dream

To Angil and Andy, for building worlds and businesses with me now, and for many years to come

Table of Contents

Introduction 1
Geography & Climate 5
    Map Making... 7
    Mountains, Coasts, and Continents 9
    Moons and Tides 13
    The Compass, the Equator, and the Poles 15
    Rivers, Lakes, and Other Small Bodies of Water 17
    Forests, Plains, and Swamps 20
    Settlements and Roads... 22
    Diversity and Tension... 26
        Example: Evolution of the Shard Map......... 27
Building Settings 31
    Earth as a Futuristic Setting.................................. 33
        Example 1: The Rose Garden....................... 35
        Example 2: The Underground 38
Species.. 39
    Race vs Species 39
    Language 41
    Life Span 45
    Humans and Humanoids.. 47
        Humans 47
        Aliens 48
        Dwarves 50
        Elves 50
        Fair Folk, Fae, and Fairies 51
        Trolls, Ogres, and Orcs.................................. 51
        Demons, Angels, Spirits................................. 52
        Vampires, Shape Shifters 53
    Non-Humanoid Sentient Species 55
        Dragons 55
        Unicorns 56

Talking Animals, Familiars, Animal Spirits .. 57
Magical and Technical Entities 58
Non-Sentient Species 59
Importance of Diversity 61
    Example 1: From Giants to Fairies 66
    Example 2: The Alarans Pt. 1 68
Cultures 69
Societal Age and Tech Levels 71
Class and Caste Structure 77
Religion 85
Political and Legal Systems 89
Job/Education 94
Interaction Between Species/Cultures 98
Magic and/or Technology Usage 100
The 'Unimportant' Stuff 110
History 116
    Example 1: The Alarans, Pt. 2 118
    Example 2: An Underground Utopia 121
Characters 125
Names and Identifiers 125
Physical Appearance and Attributes 127
Cultural Background 132
Family 134
Home – Past and Present 140
Religion/Beliefs 141
Job/Education 144
Preferences 147
Personality and Quirks 149
Abilities/Disabilities/Talents 151
    Example 1: Angel of Light 154
    Example 2: The Five Rose Princesses 156
From World Building to Story Writing 161
Bibliography 173
Worksheets 175
    Sample Character Profile - Physical 176

Sample Character Profile – Extended.......... 177
Sample Character Profile – Backstory 178
Sample Species/Culture Physical Profile.... 180
Sample Species/Culture Details 181
Sample Setting Profile - Countries 183
Sample Setting Profile – Cities/Towns 184
Sample Setting Profile – Individual Location 186
Character Profile - Physical 188
Character Profile – Extended 189
Character Profile – Backstory 190
Character Interview Questions 191
Species/Culture Physical Profile 200
Species/Culture Details 201
Setting Profile - Countries 202
Setting Profile – Cities/Towns 203
Setting Profile – Individual Location 204
About the Author 205
About Schreyer Ink Publishing 206
Also Available from Schreyer Ink 207
Coming Soon 209

Introduction

There are lots of books on writing. There are books on the craft of writing, the technical aspects of writing, on the business end of writing, on marketing your writing. There are books on characters, language, setting, and every possible genre. I'm certain there are even books on world building.

I learned to build worlds by doing two things – reading books and building worlds.

I started world building the way many writers do – I took a series I loved and started tinkering with the world that author had built. For me, that was the world of Redwall Abbey, a delightful series by Brian Jacques. That was in junior high. I have also tinkered with the world in Tamora Pierce's Wild Magic and Alanna series, and with the fantasy world of Laurel K Hamilton's Nightseer, over the years, just for practice.

In high school I tried my hand at original worlds. The first that was even moderately successful (if by moderately successful we mean 'it didn't have too many glaring plot holes' and not 'I finished a book set in this world and published it to great critical acclaim') was an urban fantasy with vampires and demons and the devil. Can you tell I was a teenager at the end of the millennium? I even threw in some mob-boss style political aspirations. I've yet to see a book where a vampire is elected president of the United States of America. I've also yet to revisit, rebuild, and rewrite this series.

What really sparked my passion for world building was Zoedar. I will talk a lot about Zoedar in this book. You can look for Zoedar all you want, it doesn't exist yet, not outside my notebooks anyways. It's a long-term back-burner project, one that I have been working on in some way since I was sixteen.

Zoedar originally belonged to my best friend, Stephanie. She allowed me to step into this world with her and allowed me to build with her. Over the years Zoedar evolved and continues to evolve. We added and removed entire fantasy species. We shifted the plot, sometimes in small ways, sometimes so drastically entire characters and plot lines had to be dropped. Characters changed names, changed relationship to each other, changed place of origin, and changed abilities.

The more I learn about world building the stronger this imaginary world becomes.

There is something about world building that makes it difficult to teach. For one thing, it is not a linear process, and many aspects are tightly interwoven with each other. For another, there is no real "right" order to work in. And then there's the added complication of genre and sub-genre and how it changes what we as writers need in, and what our readers expect from, a fictional world.

I don't have a single path or order that I follow when building a world, it all depends on where my inspiration comes from. If I were to record my creation process it would be a higgley-piggley mess and of no use to anyone who is looking for assistance or a creative resource.

Instead I have tried to layout the chapters in a way that will make it easy for you to find and reference the information you need. There are some steps that are easier to do before or after another step but overall, don't worry if you don't do things in the order in which I do them, or the order in which I've outlined them here.

I read and write a lot of fantasy, with science-fiction a close second. I have tried to make this book a valuable resource for any genre, from historic fiction, to urban speculative fiction, to all sub-genres of fantasy and sci-fi.

For historic fiction writers, this resource will help you pinpoint the details you need to research as you build an immersive and 'accurate' historic setting for your story. You'll be researching more than you are creating, though there will be times you'll need to fill in the gaps in the available knowledge with your best guess. And this book should help you make the best guesses possible based on what you know of the time and culture you're writing about.

For science fiction you'll focus more on technology levels than magic but building an alien planet for your space-faring characters to explore is very similar to building a fantasy planet. For those writing near-future Earth-based sci-fi or dystopian Earth sci-fi a lot of your geography and climate will be based on current Earth and the studies into climate change or nuclear fallout, and you'll be using modern human cultures as a template.

Alien cultures and fantasy cultures will give the writer the most creative freedom, with any historic period and any existing culture open as a treasure-trove of inspiration. It also gives the writers the most room to error.

As you read through this book and work through your own world building projects, take what you need, skip over the parts that don't apply to your story, work in the order that feels right for you, adapt questions and examples to suit your needs, and above all, have fun.

Geography & Climate

I'm going into a fair amount of detail in this chapter. You see, while we write fiction and it doesn't really matter where our cities are built or what direction the river flows, it does matter a little. You can write a story where details like river direction, climate trends, and city placement, have no bearing on the plot. It's easy and quite common. For me, as a reader, I don't really care. As long as your world sounds exciting and plausible I'm not going to double check that your mountain range interacts with your rain fall patterns in a scientifically sound way. I'm betting the majority of readers don't care either.

As a writer and a world builder I'm intensely interested in how the world I'm creating works, not just the politics, but the weather and the geography as well. Floods, droughts, and other natural disasters quickly become political issues and I want to know where they might happen. I want to know who builds moats to keep armies out and who builds them to keep flood waters out. I want to know which cultures eat a lot of fish because they have access to a lot of fish and which areas hunt more because they're near a forest. This will all change how they view their deities and their politics.

Geography is a lot more than just plopping towns down on a map and throwing some rivers, forests, and mountains around them. Other things to consider are tides and currents.

Where physical landmarks are changes the climate, the weather, the resources people have access to, and the economics of a region. Most obviously your character can't be a fisherman if he doesn't live near a big enough body of water. Similarly, you don't get hurricanes in the middle of the continent. You can, however, get flash floods in the desert.

I don't want to frighten you off. The best way to start is to have your story take place in a single country in a larger world. Place that country in a similar location to the country or state or province you live in, have lived in previously, have studied extensively, or have visited often. Give your fictional place similar geographical features to where you live and similar seasonal weather patterns and it will come across as believable.

So long as your weather is plausible and follows fairly consistent, moderate patterns, your reader will be satisfied.

If the climate, weather, or physical landmarks will play a bigger role in the plot you will want to spend more time planning it out.

Map Making

If you are artistically challenged, don't panic. Your map doesn't have to be pretty, and in some cases, you don't even need a map at all. Here are some of my guidelines for deciding if a map is needed for my story:

The story contains a lot of travelling.

The story takes place before electricity and the characters are sending messages over long distances.

The story takes place in a real place and I want a sense of accuracy.

If your story falls into any of these categories, you'll want a working map. This is a map for you, the writer, and it will help you to keep track of travel times. A quick outline of continents with some lines dividing countries and swirly lines for forests and wavy lines for rivers and dots for cities and you're done. Make a quick scale (I honestly use my fingers, 1 finger width on the page equals so many miles or a full day of travel), label places as people go to them and you're done.

This will help you keep your timeline in order as you write. You can look at your map to figure out how many days it will take a letter to arrive, how many blocks a person has to walk from the pub to get home, or how many weeks it will take them to cross the forest after losing their ponies. It will also help you keep track of what direction people are travelling in, and where they are located in relation to each other and major events or locations.

Many fantasy novels have maps in the front (The Hobbit, The Belgariad and The Mallorean Sagas by David Eddings, even the Mercy Thompson novels by Patricia Briggs). Some of these maps are very simple with notes from the author that they are not to scale. Others, like Tolkien's, are extremely detailed and as accurate as a work of fiction can be.

I recommend checking them out if you plan to include a version of your map in your published book. There are some technical aspects you need to keep in mind, like keeping the map simple enough that it doesn't turn into a blob when shrunk down to size. Some lines that you have on your working map (like paths characters take) are not necessary on the published map. As well, look into neatening the artwork – spirals across the page aren't going to cut it for a forest. If you don't feel confident doing it yourself, consider not publishing it (it isn't necessary, even in epic fantasy), or getting the help of an artist.

Mountains, Coasts, and Continents

Mountains are formed in chains or ranges. To have a single mountain alone in the middle of nowhere is rare. This is because mountains are generally formed by two tectonic plates colliding a pushing the ground up in a long ridge along the length of the plates.

A single mountain is formed by a volcano, generally. There are other ways. It could be a single tall volcano at the end of a mountain range and between it and the rest of the range is a region of low hills. Wind erosion can severely alter the appearance of the mountains. And of course, there's always the chance that some magical event took place, or it's a terraforming anomaly.

Just because it's a scientific rarity in our world doesn't mean you can't do it. Just have a reason for its existence ready for when a know-it-all geography student reads your book and tells you why you're wrong.

In Zoedar there is a spire of rock in the middle of the plains, several days away from the coastal mountains. It's all that's left of an ancient, and rather small mountain range. The last of the mountain range was dismantled by people building Caprex, the city around the spire, and The Flying Kingdom, the castle built at the top of the spire.

The following picture is not to scale:

A shoreline is anywhere that land meets water. A coast is generally a shoreline where the edge of a continent meets the ocean.

Continents are just giant flat-topped mountains sticking out of the ocean. At least in our world. And a coast is how high up the slope of the land the water can come before there just isn't anymore water.

Coasts are not smooth, but you can draw them as smooth for your reference maps. Coasts can slope down gently into the water, or they can be giant cliffs. They can be sandy or rocky or muddy clay.

Often cities or villages are built along coasts because they provide transportation and access to fish or seals or other marine animals. As well, sea weed, shells, and other resources can come from the water and be used for all sorts of things like baskets, mats, jewelry, etc. Sheltered bays or high cliffs provide water access while still being defensible against attack.

These are the land masses and boundaries that will make up the largest parts of your world. They also have a large role to play in climate and weather patterns.

Storms and rainfall follow specific patterns. Warm wet air from the coast cools as it goes up the mountains. Cold wet air makes rain or snow. One side of your mountains will always get more rain than the other.

Coasts will be battered by severe rains but inland can face high winds. Dry regions are prone to fires.

Regions near mountains or canyons can be prone to earthquakes.

Proximity is also a factory. There are two continents on Zoedar that are separated by a relatively narrow channel. The severity of the tides rushing in and out of this channel would have made this region unpassable, except that Zoedar has three moons which makes the tides more flexible and less severe than on Earth. Still, this is a treacherous passage to traverse by ship and is full of odd rip-tides.

Moons and Tides

That neatly brings us to this next section. Yes, how many moons you have, the size of them, and their proximity to your planet, will alter your weather and climate patterns.

Our moon is responsible for our tides. The gravitational pull of the moon on the earth's surface tugs on the oceans. For the most part this will only be useful as a plot device. Have you ever considered tying someone down on the beach? The clock is ticking. In a few hours the tide will rush in and the beach will be under six feet of water. How will they escape? Or how will the hero make it there to rescue them in time?

Aside from that, and the example I mentioned before about impassible storm channels, the other thing to keep in mind is that the tides affect the direction of the water currents.

The East Atlantic Current brings warm water up the coast of Spain and continues North past the United Kingdom. It cools as it reaches England then picks up cold water along Greenland's southern tip and pushes that down past the coast of Newfoundland and New England. It warms slightly as it reaches New York and continues warming as it heads South towards the equator, eventually looping Northward again and heading back towards Spain.

This current plays a huge roll in the weather in several regions. Any change to the direction, speed, or temperature of this current will change the weather everywhere along its path.

If a moon is larger, or closer, it will create stronger tides. The water will rush in towards the coast and away from the coast faster and with more force (causing more erosion in the process).

If you have more than one moon each moon will exert its own pull on the oceans. This means mini-tide shifts more times throughout the day, less severe or sudden tidal shifts, and much stranger water flow patterns.

Of course, this is an example of something that isn't going to be in the book at all, except as a passing description about the glory of the crashing tide, unless you're writing a natural disaster adventure science fiction novel, or as a plot device to provide a natural ticking clock.

The Compass, the Equator, and the Poles

Even when building Alien worlds, for science fiction or fantasy, there are some aspects of English we tend to maintain for simplicity's sake. Year. Week. Day. North, south, east, west. Doesn't matter what planet you're on, the compass means relatively the same thing.

Again, there are times when stranding a science fiction crew on a planet where their compasses don't work at all, is going to be useful to you as a plot device. For the most part though, stick to the directions people are familiar with.

You're going to have a North and South Pole, or equivalent thereof, on your planet. This is simply the point where the rotational axis of your planet is located.

Going around the middle of your planet will be your equator. Generally, if your planet spins on an axis and orbits a heat-generating star, your axis are going to be cooler with more extreme seasonal shifts and your equator is going to be warmer with fewer seasonal shifts. The size and tilt of your planet, size of your sun, proximity of the two to each other, amount of water, and layout of continents will determine how different the weather at the equator is from the weather at the poles.

Most readers are going to expect the weather to get cooler going North or South away from the equator and get warmer as they head towards the equator. Unless a completely different weather pattern or planetary design is crucial to your plot, I'd stick with this basic model.

That being said, Terry Pratchet's Disc World, and Bungie's Halo have non-spherical planetary construction with their own unique weather and climate patterns. You really can do anything you want as long as you have a plausible reason for how/why it works and keep it consistent.

Rivers, Lakes, and Other Small Bodies of Water

Water follows certain physical laws, such as gravity. Water gathers in low points, it flows from high to low, and it falls from the sky. Enchanted or magically generated water sources, or water sources that have been tampered with using advanced technology may be exempt from natural physical laws.

Lakes, ponds, and catch basins or flood plains are easy. These are low spots. Rain water and spring run off gathers here and sits. Large, low areas will turn into swamps which I'll cover in the next section.

Rivers and streams are more complicated. First, they always flow downhill. Gravity. Rivers always flow into each other, they do not diverge without good reason. Flowing water follows the path of least resistance. If there's a rock in the way it will go around, but generally just to one side or the other. A sudden rise in water levels that causes a river to overflow its bank at a key location causing enough erosion could cause a divergence, and human interference can cause divergence, but generally water follows one path.

Streams flow into rivers. Rivers flow into ponds or bays or oceans. Water doesn't flow out of ponds or rivers or oceans. If it does then you don't really have a lake, you have a wide, slow moving, stretch of river. That's not to say that a mountain lake won't overflow its banks and feed a river every time it rains. Often a water source, like an underground spring, creates a pool around itself through erosion, and that pool drains into the river which then follows the path of most gravitational pull and least resistance towards sea level or a drainage basin.

Now that we've covered how and were to draw the rivers on your map, here's why rivers and lakes are important.

Before steam engines they allowed us to move stuff that was too heavy for people or horses to pull, even with wheels. Barges pulled by horses on the shore can move huge pieces of rocks downstream, or even up stream, from quarry to building site.

They provide food. Not just fish or shell fish, which live in the water, but animals and birds that come to the water for food and drink. Rivers are rich hunting grounds.

They provide other resources such as reeds or clay, which are important for pre-plastic civilizations.

They provide water.

They provided a faster mode of travel than horses or wagons, in some cases. And often it was a safer mode of travel as you did not risk running into wolves.

They provide a natural and easily enforced boundary between clans, races, or species.

They move water which prevents flooding.
They power water wheels for grain mills. They power hydro dams, a relatively clean, though not consequence free, source of electricity.

Because waterways were so important to pre-electricity, pre-modern cultures water was often an important religious symbol. Places of worship might be located near water, there may be a deity of rain, rivers, or aquatic animals, or water may be the symbol of a deity or weather or fertility.

Forests, Plains, and Swamps

Since we've just finished with other waterways, let's look at swamps. Swamps are created with rivers find too many paths or no path at all, and there isn't enough of a low spot to create a lake or pond. A large area of low-lying ground becomes saturated with ground water and run-off.

Swamps are crucial to our ecosystems. They act like the filter in a Brita jug. The dirty water flows down the river, gets caught in the tangle that is the swamp, and relatively clean water flows out.

The shallow, slow moving, or stagnant waters provide homes from numerous animals, which in turn provide food for a lot of birds. This is a breeding ground for insects as well.

Swamps tend to be humid, muggy, muddy places that most people avoid. But they are a source of peat moss (a good fertilizer) and may be home to plants or animals your cultures require for medical or magical purposes.

Plains are dry swamps – large flat areas of grass and shrubs. The savannahs in Africa, cattle country USA, the bread basket of Canada, these are all types of plains. These regions may be good for farming or hunting but there is little shelter here.

Take if from a Canadian Prairie girl, when the winds blow there is nothing for miles to stop it.

Winters here are cold, dry, and windy. The heat can be unbearable on a plain because of lack of shade and without ample water sources they can turn into deserts. Wind erosion is a real risk, which is what makes wild grasses so important. The root system of grass prevents the erosion of soil from wind or water and prevents the soil from drying out in the sun too quickly.

If you have horse or cattle-based cultures, you'll rely on plains a lot.

Forests are large groups of trees. There are different types of forests depending on climate and type of trees.

Forests provide oxygen recirculation as well as shelter for animals, a natural wind break, and resources. They are coveted areas of land but also dangerous.

The quality of soil, amount of wind and water, and overall annual temperature patterns will determine what type of trees you have, how large they are, and how tightly packed they are. Often you start with a thin, scraggly forest of evergreens on the side of a mountain. As it gets lower, out of the rocky soil and into richer, deeper soil, you get healthier trees and more variety in plant life.

Forests shelter predators as well as prey and in dry years can fall victim to forest fires.

Settlements and Roads

In the real world we build towns and cities because there's a good reason to settle down in a specific spot. Good resources and good defences are high on the list of reasons to build a settlement.

Farming regions are settled in a spread-out fashion, generally with two or three houses close together and surrounded by the farm land each person owns. Then the next cluster, then the next. In a central location a market may spring up so that the farmers can come in and trade with each other and with travellers. If the market grows large enough you may get an inn, then a black smith and a ferrier. And slowly the town will grow.

Fishing villages, mining villages, and wood cutter towns all grow in the same way – close to a resource and built around the market that supports the workers.

Some towns grow around keeps, castles, or monasteries. If you have serfs or slaves or really poor peasants who can't own land, then you'll have towns like these. The keep is where the land owner lives. Outside his walls the market town will spring up where all his serfs work and trade and live. Spread out around that will be his pasture and farm land and the forest that provides his wood and game. Sometimes, instead of a keep, you'd have a monastery or other religious site. The members of the religious order might rent out the land they own to peasant farmers. A market would spring up to support the farmers and the pilgrims coming through town.

As your culture evolves away from a feudal system the location of the towns doesn't change, just the size and layout until you have modern towns and cities. There are remains of the old trading forts in Winnipeg, and there are other cities, especially in Europe, where the keep, castle, or monastery still stands, if only as a historic site.

Waterways were the fastest roads available. Barges, boats, and rafts were the most economical way of moving goods, with or against the current. Water was also essential for people and livestock. The majority of your towns will be within a day's easy walk of a sustainable and reliable water source, be it a river, lake, or well.

Roads weren't straight until we got our hands on dynamite. Roads, like rivers, followed the path of least resistance. They crossed rivers, mountains, and forests at the easiest points. They meandered across the landscape. Roads going through a town might be paved but most "highways" between towns were not.

The upkeep of roads and bridges depended on taxes gathered from land owners, and from trade. The wealthier a region was in resources and trade the better the roads were likely to be. And the closer the roads were to the person handling those taxes, the better the roads were.

Upkeep was more than just paving and potholes and keeping the bridges passable, it also meant security for travellers. If bandits made a road unsafe it could reroute trade or halt it all together. Roads and settlements were policed by conscripted soldiers, or by sell swords. Either way, that money generally came out of those same taxes, and only when the danger posed by the bandits put enough financial pressure on the lords.

Your politics may be different, so your road quality and safety may be better or worse. You may be dealing with intergalactic travel instead of pre-steam engine travel. The same mindset and logic applies.

Your characters will want to take the cheapest, easiest route from point A to point B. You build your settlements where you can easily build roads, have access to water and other resources, and can defend yourself. This holds true whether you're in a feudal era fantasy or you're terraforming a planet.

For space travel you'll want to consider things like orbital space stations, where on the planet ships can land (they're generally pretty big things), and obstructions such as asteroid belts and space debris or radiation from celestial events.

With space travel you gain speed, but you also gain expenses – specifically a fuel source, and finding people qualified to fly these expensive and complicated pieces of equipment. On the flip side, a barge is slow, but most commoners who grew up along a river would know how to use one.

If you're writing a more contemporary setting with established cities keep in mind that once we started settling in closer to each other grids became the norm. Straight lines are a sign of a successful and well-thought-out city. Older districts won't be so straight because old landmarks sit in odd places.

Again, ease of travel is paramount. That's why we build over passes and underpasses and put up street lights and street signs. Shopping centres appear with regularity, so people have access to resources. Water and sewage management are important to the health of the citizens.

Look at the city you live in, or cities in climates similar to the one you are writing, for ideas on architectural styles and weather proofing.

I've focused mostly on past-inspired settings here, and I've expanded that to cover futuristic cities in the "Earth as a Futuristic Setting" section.

Diversity and Tension

A diverse landscape is required IF you're creating an entire world. If your story takes place on a star ship or in a single country, you may not need this much geography. If you don't live on a coastline you don't have to worry about figuring out how the characters deal with hurricanes or laws regarding sea trade. If you don't have a forest in your country, you need to mention where the wood is imported from, but only if it's important to the plot. Most readers will simply assume that there's a source of wood nearby that you haven't mentioned, or that they trade for it, and keep reading.

Your geography can be more than just background, it can be used to create tension. Going on a quest is more exciting when you must climb mountains and battle great forest monsters. Different types of terrain or bad weather can slow characters down and an approaching deadline combined with unforeseen road blocks (oh no, a flash flood washed out that bridge we need!) builds tension without adding violence to a story. As well, one of the major plot types is man vs nature. Being left alone in the woods or mountains in severe weather can be terrifying.

Your forest or swamp may be home to monsters or spirits. Your geographical layout may breed severe storms. The possibilities are endless.

Example: Evolution of the Shard Map

When I started this map I very little idea of what I needed or wanted from this world. I tried looking for random map generators online but the only ones I could find were for dungeon masters building RPG campaigns.

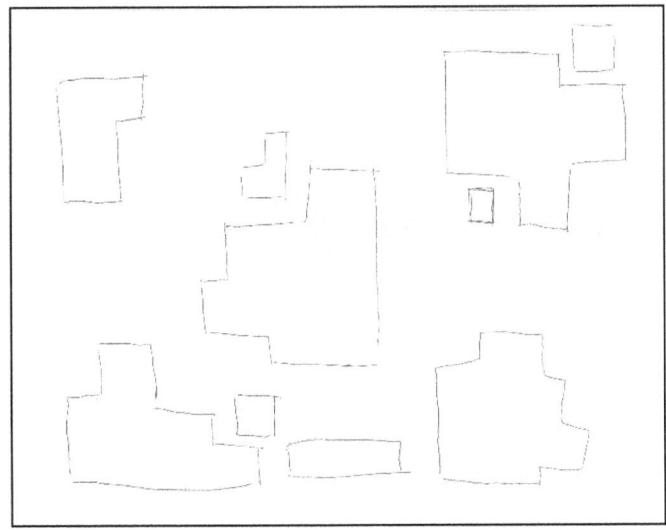

I used the random dungeon generator and drew in some of the rooms, leaving out the hallways. This left me with a very boxy map, but it was a start.

I put a piece of scrap paper over this map and started making the edges more land-like and adding reefs and mountains.

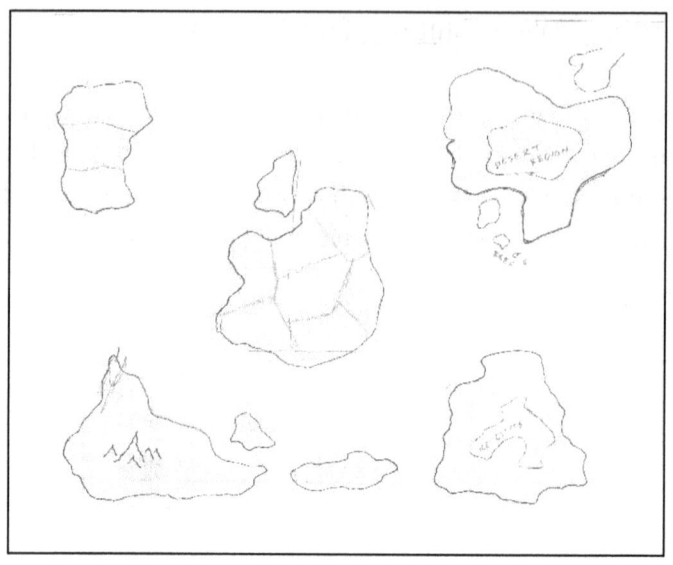

I had two or three copies of the map at this stage on which I could sketch the locations of cities, trade routes, and borders, and note things like travel time.

This map was enough for my personal use while writing, but with all the notes and scribbles, and the fact that you can still see what was on the flip side of the paper, it's not a map that could be used in a published book.

I traced this map again and made a copy with the same style of shading as the old sepia maps that would be hung on study walls as works of art, not just as functional tools of navigation.

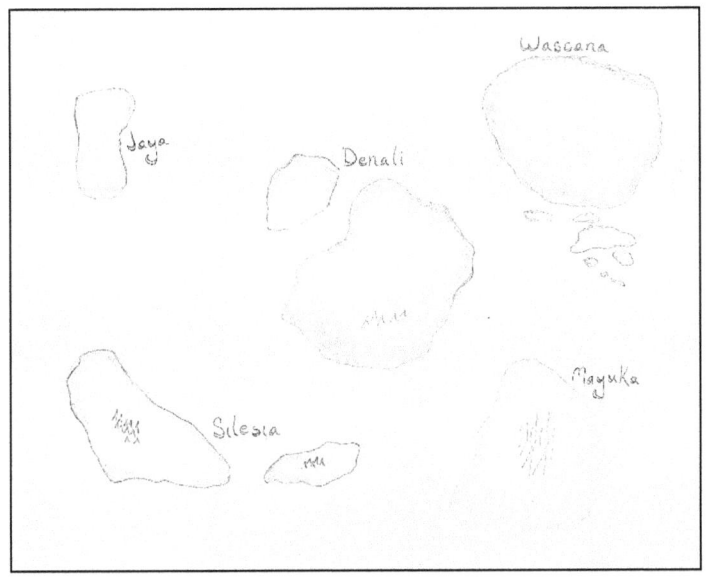

The only things that need to be added to this map before it could be used in a novel are a scale and compass, and the location of major cities. I haven't added those yet because the world and the stories in it are undergoing a major overhaul and the names and locations of borders, countries, and cities will be changing quite a bit.

Building Settings

You have three major puzzle pieces when building a story: plot, character, and setting. Plot is what happens, character is who the plot happens to, and setting is where the plot takes place. In the simplest of terms, anyway.

Much of your world building is going to help you build your settings, the concrete places in which the scenes of your story will take place. Yes, in part, this is the countries and continents you're building, but more specifically it's the church buildings, the towns, the castles, the forest camps, and other such sets.

Not only is setting individual, concrete locations, but also the concrete, specific details that we choose to describe these locations. Saying 'a forest' is one thing. Saying 'a dark, dense forest of ancient oaks' is far more interesting. Use tight, specific, direct language when crafting your setting. This will help create a vivid sense of place, and, if you choose carefully, can help you avoid info dumps.

As you were building your cultures you probably borrowed from several real-world religious and political systems. You will continue to borrow from various real-world and fictions settings now.

You've selected a societal age and tech level. This will narrow down the architectural choices you have for the style of your buildings and the size and layout of your villages or cities. If you're writing a Victorian steampunk, for example, your physical setting will be based heavily on Victorian London, or Victorian-era Paris, or Prague or whichever city best suits your story. Onto that base you'll add your steampunk technology, tweaking the style of clothes and décor and buildings to fit the additions.

If you're writing a period fantasy set in a blend of Feudal and Late-Middle-Ages with heavy European leanings you're looking at castles and moats with villages springing up around their walls. You're looking at placing major cities near waterways, in strategically defensible positions, or near key resources. For architecture you'll want to peak at period appropriate buildings around the world and blend them together. Keep in mind that without magic you're stuck with building techniques that fit your technology level.

Earth as a Futuristic Setting

Writing science-fiction can pose a unique challenge, especially if set on Earth. You have a setting that is familiar, and yet you must make it different. You look at the current state of environmental affairs and you must project a likely path into the future.

Rising tides? Nuclear war? An earthquake finally turns California into an island? A volcanic eruption? Whatever the case, something happens and the world changes. Maybe it's not environmental, maybe the change is political. Maybe the change is in population density, or technology.

There are many classic examples, but two movies come to mind: Blade Runner, and Johnny Mnemonic. In both of these we see futuristic settings that combine high tech gadgets with crumbling infrastructure. Both vividly show that while things progress ever faster for the wealthy, the poor live much as they always have and progress for them comes much slower.

At the same time, Star Trek gives us an example of a clean, shiny future Earth where poverty has been eradicated and no one wants for anything. This points to a fundamental split in science-fiction. On the one hand is fiction that gives us a look at "if we keep making these bad choices we'll end up somewhere like this", while on the other hand we see "what can happen if we get our act together and live up to our full potential". Honestly,

I think there is a place for both types of science fiction. We need both the cautionary tale and the hopeful tale. Of course, they require two very different settings.

If you take a walk through a major European city, you'll see buildings that are older than my country (Canada is only 150 years young!) across the street from shiny modern buildings of steel and glass. Unless there's a reason for a building to be torn down (disdain for old things, structural instability, major event that levels entire city streets) your cities will be a blend of old and new buildings.

Often you have historic districts as the city will grow in sections, each section modelled on the period it was built in. We see that in homes, this suburb has all bungalows with detached, 1-car garages, the next neighbourhood has attached 2-car garages with the room over the garage. As the city expands each suburb has a different style.

You will have areas that are industrial and areas that are residential. You'll have areas that are old stone and areas that are newer.

And all this can translate over to alien civilizations as well. If they are space faring beings, their civilization is likely centuries old, and will have a rich and varied history that will include an evolution of building materials and architectural styles.

Example 1: The Rose Garden

In the Rose Garden series, I have five provinces, each of which follows a different spirit guide. The five provinces are allies, and people can live outside the province of their cultural origins. Each book takes place in one of the five provinces and focuses on one of the five princesses. I had to develop five different sets of settings for this series.

In book one the story takes place in the Stone Clan province. The castle is solidly built with heavy walls and small windows. Their décor of choice is mainly statues and pottery. The masonry work on the pillars is exquisite. All the roads in the capital are paved with cobble stones. The temple has a mosaic on the floor.

The keep she visits is also solidly built with the trademark heavy walls and small windows. Bannisters are stone. Some of the benches are stone. There's a pattern here.

She also visits a mining camp where, because of cost and other factors, the men live in tents, or travel up from the village at the base of the mountain. The camp has a different feel, but the solid stone presence is still there, this time in the form of the mountain.

In book two I move the story to the Sun Temple province. There, the temple and castle are more open with larger windows. While there is still a mosaic in the main temple, there are also stained-glass windows everywhere, and lots of candles.

The library is one of the major settings and it is a grand room with different levels and lots of shelves and tables. Some back corners are dark, but this physical darkness is balanced with the sense of freedom the princess feels while there.

The bank and the guild halls are described as luxurious, richly decorated, and extravagant. There is the feeling of being in the economic and cultural center of the island.

I'm working on book three which will take place in Evergrowth. This is a province of plants, of farmers and woodsmen and healers. There is a lot more wood construction here, instead of stone. There are open gardens, window box planters, and ivy-covered walls. Here wealth is shown not in the size of the building, or the money, or the books, but in well-kept yards, fine fabrics, and elaborate tapestries.

As the series moves to the province of the Animal People the focus will shift to pets and to leather and to a sense of physical fitness – people who are strong and fleet and graceful. Here music and dance are at the heart of creative expression.

Finally, the series moves to the province of the Metalkin. Here strength is shown in iron and finery in gold and silver. The people here are haughty, even arrogant, and many of the wealthy are hard and uncaring.

Here is where the twists and turns of the story come together to be hammered out and set to rights.

To create these settings, the castles and capital buildings, the keeps and camps, I took what I know of the people I was creating, their technology levels, their economic structures, their political history, the education and courtship rituals of the upper class, and I combined all that to create a unique sense of place for each of the five provinces.

Example 2: The Underground

In the Underground books there is one basic setting: an underground megacity. While some of the characters get to see more than one of these megacities they are all essentially the same. There are lots of lights and the walls are white giving the illusion of space but also creating a bland, almost sterile environment. Public spaces are lined with advertisement, like our subway stations and bus stops. The lifts have screens that play the news and advertisements to passengers. Everything is brightly coloured.

To counteract the coldness of the halls I created a coziness within the communities and families. Sure, they have a small apartment, but it often smells of cookies or stew and is filled with the sounds of kids playing together. The teens can visit the arcade or the pool whenever their schedules allow to spend time with friends and classmates. Both these places are full of life and people and noise.

Again, I took everything I had outlined about technology, education, and political history and translated it into a physical space.

Species

Race vs Species

Here on Earth this is an easy distinction to make. A species is a unique type of animal. Some are related to each other in that they evolved from a common ancestor but, with only one or two exceptions, species have evolved away from each other to the point where they can no longer interbreed and produce offspring. Race, on the other hand, is a social construct designed to divide humans into categories based on where they come from or the colour of their skin.

Traditionally fantasy writers in particular have used race to mean different species of humanoids and sentient non-humanoids (elves, halflings, humans, dragons, unicorns, orcs, trolls …). This is problematic for several reasons. By using race and species interchangeably in our writing we reinforce the idea that some people are naturally better at certain things than others simply because of where they are born (elves are better at magic, dwarves are better smiths, etc.) and that some people are naturally evil (dark elves, orcs, trolls).

In this book I'll be referring to different types of creatures as species and different traditions within a species as cultures, leaving out the word race entirely. How you label the "people" in your world is up to you.

At this stage you're selecting which species you want to include in your world and choosing their base physical attributes. This means their height ranges (human males range in height from four-foot-four to eight feet but average between five and a half and six and a half, human females tend to be shorter than males, on average), possible hair and eye colours, fantasy elements such as wings, odd shaped ears, etc., supernatural physical abilities (levitation, laser eyes, super strength, etc.), and magical abilities. You'll build their religion, culture, and society later.

I tend to do one species from creation to completion, so this stage and the culture stage, before starting the next species on my list. You can do it that way or do all the physical attributes for all the races first and then build all their cultures afterwards if you choose.

Don't be afraid to come back and add or change things. You'll come across interesting tidbits in articles or stories as you're world building and will want to include them in some way. This happens to me all the time. As well, as your cultures begin to interact with each other you'll find there are parts of their societies that need more details, or no longer make sense.

I recommend reading articles on ancient civilizations, as well as current politics, and literary analysis. I've found inspiration in all these places.

Language

There are dozens of languages and hundreds of dialects on Earth alone. It makes sense that every culture will have a different language. It also makes sense that your reader will not want to learn a new language every time they pick up a new book or meet a new culture in a series they're already reading.

There are resources available for creating your own language (referred to as a Conlang) for fictional races, and it can be fun to do, but using your created language in your story should be done sparingly.

Here are some tricks for including species and races with different languages in your story, and for including Conlang in your story:

Simply mentioning that characters are speaking a language that the main characters can't understand. "Matt watched as the alien bounty hunters discussed the deal in Nubian. He didn't understand the words but from their facial expressions he could tell they were interested."

Using it in small doses and translating it right away. "The elf trader said, 'Ha mina ju haster.' Jeffery turned to his father. 'He says we can have the wheat for fourteen silvers.'"

Using Conlang for rituals and ceremonies. The exact words of a ceremony aren't always important, so this is a good place to add a little fantasy or alien flavour without sacrificing readability.

Using Conlang for magical artifacts or special technology, things that don't have a name in English to begin with. Since you're making up a name for the item anyways, feel free to make that name reflect your fantasy or alien race.

Using alien or fantasy sounding names for characters.

Whichever route you take, use fantasy or alien languages sparingly as you would any other complicated or specialty terminology.

Something else to consider is slang and swearing. Some casual language is pretty safe to use, like "shut up", but other phrases are culturally or time-period specific. Like any reference to Jesus as a swear word – a world with no form of Christianity won't swear that way.

"My legs feel like Jell-O." Is that possible in a world that doesn't have Jell-O? Solving this could be as simple as replacing Jell-O with jelly, since most cultures had some form of preserved fruit spread, or replacing it with "wobbly" or "weak".

Any slang that uses a brand name or modern product, or a person, place, or thing that doesn't exist in your fictional society has to be replaced by something the characters would be familiar with.

If they don't have a "hell" then every swear-phrase using that word (what the hell, who the hell, go to hell …) has to be altered. "Oh my god" might be replaced by "By the gods" – a common phrase in period-fantasy.

Timekeeping is another place where, on the one hand, you can make up words, especially for the days of the week, but at the same time you'll use a lot of Earth words and concepts, like a day, a week, a month, a year, an hour, etc.

You may want to change the names of your days from Monday, Tuesday, etc. to something more fitting to your story. Naming days after gods or celestial bodies/events is common and precisely how we ended up with Thursday (Thor's Day) and Sunday (literally Sun Day).

You can change the names of your months as well. In the Rose Garden books the months are Cloudrise, Hoofrise, Thornrise, Daggerrise, Starrise, Cloudfall, Hooffall, Thornfall, Daggerfall, Starfall, and Holy Week.

You can change the number of days in your week, the number of weeks in your month, the number of days/months in your year – but you need to be clear about this when you're writing.

Again, to use Rose Garden as an example, there are 10 months, each with 36 days, or six weeks of six days each. Holy week is an oddity in that it has 5 days and marks the new year. I avoid the word 'week' in the narrative since their weeks and our weeks are not the same length.

If you're writing science fiction, timekeeping becomes even more interesting because you're dealing with space travel, multiple planets, light speed, etc. If you're working with lightspeed, black holes, gravity wells, etc. you will want to research how these phenomena affect our perception of time. If you want a well-written example I recommend Interstellar.

Life Span

You may automatically thing of Elves and other "Long Lived Races" but that's not the only reason I want to bring up life span here. Life span changes, not only based on species, but on era.

Minor injuries were much more serious to cultures that didn't have antibiotics, or basic cleanliness. We survive much today, with a few stitches, an alcohol swab, and a needle, that killed people only a few hundred years ago.

In historic fiction this is crucial. It is also crucial if you have a space faring people encounter a primitive culture. Magically enhanced healing is going to change how this works so let's stick to non-magic worlds for a moment.

When writing historical fiction keep in mind that people died all the time. Like ALL the time. Fell off a horse. Stabbed in the foot with a pitchfork. Caught the flu. Worked too long in the rain in October. Dead. All of them.

Flus, plagues, pneumonia, injuries of all sorts, work place accidents, giving birth – they happened, A LOT. And people died.

There were no unions or safety boards protecting farmers or even factory workers. In 1919 (less than one hundred years ago) Winnipeg (a city in central Canada) all but shut down for a month as approximately 30,000 people walked away from their jobs. They were striking for union protections.

People who lived prior to the 1900s died of things we don't even bat an eye at. It wasn't until the mid 1800s that we began pasteurizing milk. And it wasn't until the 1930s that indoor plumbing reached rural areas of North America.

If you have Elves or other species that are long-lived, how do they combat things like the flu? Or the infection of injuries? What is their maternal care like that they don't have women dying in childbirth by the hundreds or thousands?

Magic does change how these things work. You may be able to magically cure diseases or fix broken bones in a matter of hours instead of weeks. This raises the question of who has access to healers of sufficient training and talent? And what does it cost?

There will be a difference in the care that a poor farmer receives compared to what the liege lord receives, whether the healing is magical or not.

And magic can only cure you if a healer can reach you. How many healers are there? How much training do they need? Can everyone reach them easily? Bad weather might hinder a character's ability to reach a healer in time (and thus build tension into your story or keep magic from breaking your plot).

Humans and Humanoids

We relate most easily to characters who are most like us. Perhaps that is why the majority of sentient fantasy and science fiction species we come across in fiction walk on two legs, have an even number of limbs with some form of opposable digits on the ends, and have some form of facial features in relatively the same configuration as ours.

There is no real end to this list and I've stuck to generic, traditional creatures, leaving out story, series, or game specific creatures like Halo's Elites or James Cameron's Na'avi.

<u>Humans</u>
While these will be the most recognizable, physically, there is no end to what you can do with them culturally. Just looking at our own history you will see a huge variety of cultures and beliefs to play with.

Keep in mind that humans naturally come in a variety of shapes, sizes, and colours, and that these attributes are dependent on the geography and climate of their ancestral homes as well as their lifestyle and genetics.

Feel free to mix an match. The humans in your story who look like our Asians might have a culture styled after the Native Americans. Your Caucasian people may have an African based culture. You can even mix cultural and religious elements from many different places to create your own.

Aliens

Aliens can take a lot of forms, as popular sci-fi franchises have shown us. They can be humanoid or not, sentient or not.

Many fantasy races have long traditions behind them but aliens, well you can do anything you want with aliens.

There are two categories of sentient aliens in science fiction – the ones more advanced than humans, be they threatening or helpful, and the ones less advanced than humans, the ones we stumble upon on our travels. Some science-fiction is about exploration and meeting all these aliens, some is about the war or invasion that might occur when an advanced race of aliens finds us, some is about mostly peaceful co-existence of two or more races of beings who are then thrust into some sort of plot event. I'm sure you can name big-time movies and TV series that follow each of those.

While there are really no limits to be placed on the appearance or culture of your alien race, there are some things to keep in mind:

1. Geography and climate do affect evolution, both physical and cultural.

2. There are some pretty big plot holes to avoid, unless you're writing parody stuff. Honestly, a race advanced enough to travel through space is probably medically advanced as well so while Earth germs might slow them down in the beginning, we're not looking at the flu bug ending an invasion threat. If they're going to invade, they're going to do reconnaissance first, so they'll know all about our planet so no, elephants and wolverines won't take them by surprise and if their guns can take down our tanks and aircraft they'll be fine against our natural world.
3. You should have a plausible sounding pseudo-science reason your alien tech works. They can have strange resources and metals and crystals and stuff that give their tech power, and it can be completely impossible stuff – as long as it sounds like it could work, and the aliens know how it works.
4. Aliens do give us a way to discuss things like colonialism, racism, nationalism, fanatical theocracy, and genocide without offending a real group of people. Still, it's pretty obvious when someone takes a historical event and changes one or both parties to aliens. Take inspiration from real life but take the time to make enough changes to it as well that it becomes an original story.

Dwarves

Traditionally dwarves as a fantasy race are shorter than humans and stocky. They live underground and are miners and smiths. Their talents lie in digging and forging. This description already blends physical with traditions, species with culture.

Even within this traditional framework you can do a lot with them. I've seen dwarven monarchies, dwarves with clan systems, and dwarves with a more Roman Republic sort of government. They can be loyal or petty. They can be smart with advanced culture and craftsmanship or they can be much simpler, rustic people.

Feel free to change them up. Write dwarves who aren't afraid of or scornful of surface dwellers. Write Dwarves with a more elegant culture, instead of short Vikings with a love for ale and fighting.

As well, play with their appearance. Beards are traditional but are they useful or necessary? Would they really be so stocky, or could they be slenderer?

Elves

Elves are a complicated bunch. You've got the taller, elegant, snooty elves of Peter Jackson's Middle Earth. You have more woodland sprite style elves, you have Santa's elves, and you have everything in between. Traditionally elves have longer lifespans than humans, usually by a few hundred years. They tend to be written as playful, mischievous characters related to the fae or as snooty, better-than-thou elitists.

With the amount of variety in the tradition already there is really no need to fall back on these two tropes. Add to them, alter them, and build your own unique version.

Fair Folk, Fae, and Fairies

This is a HUGE category of characters with a lot of variety and is often closely related to elves. Fairies can take many forms, from tiny winged people to the same height as humans. They can appear human, or they can have a variety of horns, hooves, and wings.

There is a tradition of two "courts" of fairies – light and dark, seelie and unseelie, summer and winter – it goes by a lot of names. If using courts, it's tradition that the "good", friendly-looking fairies like pixies, brownies, and such, belong to the "good" court while the ugly or mean fair-folk like hob-goblins, trolls, and gnomes, belong to the "bad" court.

There are many other traditions, that faeries cannot lie, that they can use special powers like glamour or magical slumbers, and have their own realm, that you can draw on for your fairies.

Trolls, Ogres, and Orcs

I mentioned for trolls in the fair-folk section, but I want to go into them more here. Trolls, ogres, orcs, and even giants, are the large, clunking, stocky, ugly creatures of the fantasy world. Generally, they aren't very nice, ranging from grumpy individuals who prefer to be alone to downright cruel creatures.

Traditionally these creatures are working against the hero in some way. Trolls at bridges, demanding tolls, ogres in dark caves, armies of orcs, giants battering down walls – it's a tradition worth breaking.

Fantasy is a deep-rooted genre and because of that there are many clichés and tropes that have developed. Some of these are interesting and worth exploring, others are tired and overdone.

I personally think it's time to change up the tropes on "these races" are good and "those races" are evil. I think more authors need to mix things up, tell stories from other points of view, and develop fantasy races beyond their clichés.

Demons, Angels, Spirits

I'm Catholic. I grew up in a Judeo-Christian tradition. There are similar beings in other religious and cultural traditions. I think literature needs to see more of that variety.

These are beings that work well in urban fantasy and paranormal thrillers and there is a long and varied tradition for each of them. The biggest advice I can give you is to be consistent and clear in your rules of engagement.

What are the rules and conditions your demons and angels must play by? How powerful are they? What or who can stop them? Honestly, it doesn't matter what rules you lay down so long as you stick to them.

Supernatural is one of my favourite television shows but I find I have no clear idea how the demons actually work. How do they get out of hell? Can they really possess anyone? At any time? One season only angels can kill angels, the next season anyone can kill an angel if they have the right sword. I think the problem here arises with the piecemeal nature of writing for television, so I recommend building your species and cultures before you start writing, setting out your rules, and then sticking to them no matter how much easier it would be to allow your characters to find a short cut around those rules.

Vampires, Shape Shifters

Vampires, werewolves, and shape shifters, as well as other undead like zombies and ghouls, are more likely to be seen in horror, at least traditionally. There is also a strong market for them in urban fantasy, paranormal thriller, and paranormal romance.

These monsters started out as the bad guys. They were the staple of Hollywood Halloween specials for decades – mainly because it was so easy to do the make-up and effects for them on the screen.

Somewhere along the way we got sympathetic monsters – the lonely, misunderstood creatures who were willing to turn their back on their violent nature to help, and even love, the humans. It was a good twist. Now it's a cliché.

Sexy werewolves and vampires abound. More often than not they are assisting the human main character against a bigger, badder character, or a rival vampire/shifter character.

These are some of the longest running and most used creatures in fiction, both on paper and on screen. And for good reason. People love them. They love to be scared of them, they love to cheer for them, they love to hate them.

You have the option of going old-school traditional with your creatures or spicing it up with newer versions or creating your own twists. You can make them good guys or bad guys. You can make them terrifying or sexy, or both. Whatever you choose, there is a market for it. Just keep your mythos, your rules and restrictions, consistent within each book or series you write.

Non-Humanoid Sentient Species

Two-legged upright is not the only physical appearance for species to adhere to. There are plenty of other life forms out there who could be sentient, whether their intelligence and ability are known to the traditionally sentient species or not. We often consider cats very intelligent, with personality and even culture, even though we have no real way of communicating with them and no proof they are sentient.

Dragons

One of the most popular by far. There are even dragon shape shifters now. But, for now I will stick with traditional dragons. They are reptiles and can vary in size from that of a house cat to the size of an apartment building. Some fly, some do not. Some breathe fire, others breathe ice or lightning or spew acid or a poisonous mist. They can be any colour under the sun, with or without wings, and with as much or as little frills, horns, and/or spikes as desired.

On Granzer, a fictional world I'm working on, the dragons are smaller, thin and long, about the height at the shoulder of a large dog but slender and easily as long as two St. Bernards standing tip to tail. They have wings and lots of frills or fans. They are mostly green.

They are sentient but have trouble talking to other races because of the shape of their mouths and tongues.

They sing beautifully, and this is the source of their magic.

Many authors have included dragons, as wise recluses, as dangerous adversaries, or as trusted mounts or companions. The size, style, and allegiance of your dragons is up to you. Just remember, it's incredibly easy to over power a dragon so that they run the risk of breaking your plot.

Unicorns

Another common creature in fantasy is the unicorn. Generally depicted as a pure white horse with a spiral horn protruding from its forehead, they are symbols of magic and purity. It is said that only a virgin can tame one, that silver will burn them, and that removing their horn will kill them. The horns are said to have magical properties. They can be delicate, graceful creatures, or large and powerful, like war horses.

I think unicorns are often passive creatures, whether they can effectively communicate with humans or not. They are hunted and need protecting and rescuing. That, and their connection to virgins is telling of their medieval European roots.

I've read some books where unicorns are quite stuck up, like The Dragon's Tooth by Holly Geely Roger Zelazny's unicorn in Unicorn Variations was almost cynical. Don't feel like you have to follow tradition.

Related to unicorns, in form at least, is the Pegasus. Originally, he was a one-of-a-kind, a creature of Greek mythology. Over time it has become less of a proper name and more of a species label for any horse with wings. While unicorns may or may not be more sentient regular horses and may or may not be able to communicate with humans, often a Pegasus is depicted as an intelligent horse with wings but with no real culture or language beyond what a normal horse would have.

Talking Animals, Familiars, Animal Spirits

Where to start? There are so many examples of this in literature, movies, TV, and video games. Anne Bishop has her Kindred, the Blood of the animal races. Sabrina the Teenage Witch had a talking cat. Elder Scrolls has a variety of guardian spirits you can summon.

Whether they are an enchanted race, your character has a special ability, they are familiars, or incorporeal companions, talking animals can provide interesting insight and humorous perspective.

Some things to keep in mind: what language do they speak? Who can hear them? Is it a physical communication or a telepathic one? Is this common knowledge or do only certain people even know these animals can talk?

Magical and Technical Entities

I think my favourite example of this is in the magical sense is Bob, the spirit that lives in the skull on Harry Dresden's book shelf in Jim Butcher's urban fantasy series. Often, like spirits, these entities have no physical form. They may be demons, spirits, or souls, or something completely magical. I would also include Wisps in this category.

Often these beings are not friendly. They are generally locked up somehow and bound by magic to be helpful, but should they get free they would not be very nice.

On the science fiction side are the AIs and robots. Again, so many franchises have given us so many varieties. Robots that speak English, or that speak in hoots and whistles, AIs that run ships or that clip into power armor, holograms of dead crew mates, and talking toasters.

I think this category leaves a lot of room to be explored, both in fantasy and in science fiction. The possibilities both for new and creative entities and for their personalities and motives are wide open.

Non-Sentient Species

Currently humans are the only sentient species on Earth though in my opinion there are a few animals (some varieties of apes, as well as ravens and dolphins) that are rapidly approaching the point of sentience. We are obviously not alone here.

I think it is critically important that your world be populated by numerous animal species. Without them your food chain will collapse. That means you need both predators and prey out in your natural world.

Apex Predators: These are the animals at the top of the food chain and generally have no natural predators, except each other and humans. Wolves and bears are the iconic examples, as well as lions, tigers, and other wild cats. In a fantasy these animals, or their made-up equivalents, provide tension while travelling or for poorer characters who must guard livestock or hunt to survive.

Minor Predators: smaller carnivores, omnivores, and scavengers like coyotes and other wild dogs, weasels, ferrets, wolverines, badgers, etc. There can be a real challenge for farmers to deal with and can become a nuisance for travellers. Rats are one of the most overlooked dangers to a historic fiction or historic inspired fantasy. They carry disease, will eat anything, can get in just about anywhere, and will attack animals many times their size, including humans, with little or no provocation. They get into pantries and grain stores and live in alleys, cellars, and anywhere that is little-used or abandoned.

Large Prey: This includes deer, elk, moose, and I'd even include geese here. They serve as the main food source for apex predators. On the domestic side this includes cattle, horses, sheep, goats, etc. They are a good source of meat, milk, leather, and horn/bone.

Small Prey: Rabbits, squirrels, chickens, grouse: basically, anything big enough to eat or use its fur but smaller than dogs. They serve as food for everything on that predator list including humans and other sentient species.

Nuisance Animals: Rodents that are too small to eat or use furs from, as well as insects, small lizards and amphibians, etc. You rarely see a party of questing adventurers complain about mosquitoes buzzing around their ears or mice in their boots in the mornings.

This entire list doesn't have to play a huge roll in the story. If you're on a space liner you may not need it at all, except to mention what types of freeze-dried meats you have in the mess hall. Still, the occasional mention about bird song in the trees, chickens in the farm yard and a complaint about weasels, or the sound of small animals rustling in the bushes, will add a layer of realism to your story.

Importance of Diversity

When I speak of diversity I mean two things: biodiversity within an ecosystem, and representation. Both are equally important.

An ecosystem needs variety to thrive. Plants, insects, herbivores, omnivores, and carnivores, of different types, will need to exist in the wild spaces of your world. In addition, there will be farm grains and domestic animals, for food, labour, or companionship, to consider. Many authors borrow heavily from reality when building their animal populations. They have rabbits and deer, wolves and wildcats, as is reasonable for the habitat and climate. They have cattle, sheep, horses, and dogs. It's up to you whether you want to transplant familiar species to your new world or invent your own.

When writing historical fiction there are some points of reference to consider. When was the horse tamed and what was it used for? The answer will be different in different parts of the world. When were animals domesticated, and which ones? Again, answers will vary by region. The potato is a sticking point in history. It wasn't always a staple of the European diet and is often included in historical fiction in periods when it would not have been eaten. (Remember there were Africans in most parts of Europe before there were potatoes).

Beyond your ecosystem, there is the diversity of your sentient species. As I said in the section on Humans, look around, we come in all shapes, sizes, and colours. We are moving away from worlds made up of nothing but Caucasian faces, and rightfully so.

Here are some things to consider when dealing with cultural diversity:

"White" shouldn't always equal superior just as "black" or "minority" or "other" shouldn't always equal savages, slaves, or less advanced.

Be careful to avoid stereotypes. Perhaps this is more important in science fiction and urban fantasy. We need to stop with the Asian Martial Arts Master and the Asian Super Genius. We need to stop with the African-American Gang Member. We don't have Chinese Laundries anymore, nor do we call them Greasy Italians or Dirty Niggers (and I apologize now for even using these terms as examples, they are not appropriate). We need to be aware of modern racial stereotypes and steer clear of them.

Stereotypes aren't limited to race/culture. Avoid stereotypes and tropes when dealing with LBGTQ+ characters as well. Your gay man doesn't have to be overly effeminate, your lesbian doesn't have to talk and act like a man. Avoid tropes like "The Predatory Gay/Lesbian/Trans", "The Tragic Gay" (where the non-hetro character dies, or their lover dies), or "The Frigid Gay" (where the non-hetro character is never shown having an interest in romance or sex). Remember that the gender and sexuality spectrum is vast and varied. Ace characters and Aro characters are grossly underrepresented and mis-portrayed when they are in a story. Please, talk to people about what experiences and portrayals are helpful and which are hurtful.

Treat any cultural imagery, symbolism, or tradition you borrow from with respect. There's a fine line between appreciation and appropriation. This is especially true with historical fiction. Do your research.

There are more religions out there than Christianity and Ancient Greek. If you are writing urban fantasy consider focusing on one of the lesser represented world religions. And remember, Muslim doesn't equal terrorist no more than Christian equals KKK or Inquisition or Crusades. Avoid the clichés and tropes. If you're building a fantasy or alien religion don't fall back on Christianity and Ancient Greece/Rome as your sole model or inspiration.

Elves, Fairies, and other such species (nymphs, dryads, pygmies, mermaids, etc.) are fictional. They do not, to the best of my knowledge, exist in the real world. Yes, they have long traditions and they have places of origin, but that really doesn't mean much. There is already so much variation in their appearance and abilities that a little more variation isn't going to hurt. So, feel free to make your fantasy people any natural or unnatural skin-tone you please.

Avoid token characters. You get your ensemble cast together and you have the one minority character, the one fantasy species character, the one gay character, the one woman, but they're backseat to your white-straight-male-hero, and you haven't really fleshed them out. They all sound and act like white-straight-male characters. Here are some tips on avoiding this:

Make your main character something other than white-straight-physically capable-male

Avoid stereotypes – women don't always have to be meek healers. The gay guy doesn't have to be girly, or creepy.

Avoid giving your minority or non-binary character a sad backstory or a doomed character arc – don't kill them

Give their character enough page time to develop their own story arc

Give them their own personality, their own voice, and their own culture and experiences and have the white-straight-male characters respect these differences and experiences

Give minority characters a crucial skill and have them be respected for it, by everyone

Have white characters call out racist or sexist background characters. Especially if you have an ensemble cast (like a fantasy quest or the crew of a star ship) they are a team, they should stand up for each other, or learn to stand up for each other as they spend more time together.

Be boldly obvious about your characters' identities. Specify that they have dark skin or a disability or identify as something other than cis-hetro. At the same time, avoid using food as a skin colour descriptor/comparison. No, you don't have to make the focus of your plot a romance just to stress that the lead character isn't straight – but you can make some fairly obvious statements (like who their gaze lingers on, or have them mention a past lover, or a current significant other). If a straight character can talk about their family back home, their sexual prowess, who they'd like to flirt with, etc. then the non-binary, non-straight character can talk about those things as well.

Diversity isn't tokenism. It isn't pandering to the snowflakes or the bleeding-heart liberals. Diversity is a fact of life. There were Africans in England before there were potatoes in England. Remember that.

Diversity in your fiction will lend realism and depth and it will only improve your readership base. If anyone tries to tell you that diversity doesn't sell, they're lying to you.

Example 1: From Giants to Fairies

On Zoedar there are eight different sentient species. Two of those species have multiple cultures.
1. Giants: Much taller than humans or elves, they live in the main mountain range in almost complete isolation. They quarry stone and bring it down the mountain to the mouth of the river where it is transported on barges downstream. They trade for foods and cloth that they cannot farm or make in the mountains.
2. Haider: My least human species. They are a hyena-human hybrid. They are furry with hyena faces. Because they are hunched it's hard to tell how tall they are, but they stand about the same height as humans.
3. Alarans: slightly taller than humans and bearing large feathered wings the Alarans live on one of the moons orbiting the planet.
4. Humans: There are three groups of humans, the Eastern humans (Tantaria), the Western humans (Zoedavian) and the Death Cult (located on Gagen). Physically they have the same height and weight ranges as humans on Earth, but with added magical abilities.
5. Elves: There are five groups of elves, descending from three tribes. There are the forest elves, urban elves, and silver elves of Massaria. There are the dark elves, those who chose the wrong side in the great war and were banished. And there are the "ghetto"

elves, the ones who live in the southern most region of the human territories. These elves have dark skin, like Africans here on Earth, not like the Drows of the Forgotten Realms.
6. Dryads: A small group of long-lived women who live in a lake in the middle of the forest separating Tantaria from Zoedar.
7. Nymphs: Cousins to the Dryads, they live in the central and southern reaches of the forest. Smaller than humans, and exclusively female, they are an odd blend of friendly and ferocious.
8. Fairies: The smallest of the species, physically, they live in the northern regions of the forest. They are fun, flighty people.

Each species has an average height range, hair and eye colours that are typical to their people, and an average life span. For every fantasy or alien species you create you need to determine these average traits, so you know if your characters are normal for who and what they are or if they're unique in some way.

Example 2: The Alarans Pt. 1

<u>Species Name</u>: Alarans (from Zoedar)

<u>Average Height</u>: Between 5'9" and 7'. As with humans, males tend towards the higher end of the height spectrum while females tend towards the shorter. Men under 6' and women over 6'6" fall outside the Alaran norm and are considered shorter or taller than average.

<u>Normal Hair Colours</u>: Same as is normal for humans but it is possible for Alarans to have natural highlights in "unnatural" colours such as pink or blue.

<u>Normal Eye Colours</u>: Same as is normal for humans but with the addition of violets and pinks.

<u>Other physical features</u>: Large feathered wings attached at their shoulders. Wings are attached at the shoulders, they extend to head height and down almost to the ground. Their wings can be white, ivory, grey, or light brown with patterning similar to owls. The alula and marginal coverts (the feathers at the bend in the wing) can be coloured to match an element (pink, red, blue, green, yellow, purple) depending on the Alaran's abilities.

<u>Abilities</u>: Each Alaran is born with a special ability, such as control over water, exceptional talent with a weapon or instrument, or a natural ability to heal.

Cultures

I used to divide my world building into sections like "religions" and "politics" and "economics" but I found the three were too intertwined to do it that way. Even if the divides I drew made sense in my mind, it didn't make sense to teach it that way, or explain it that way. So now I talk about culture as a whole.

Culture is made up of religious beliefs, holiday traditions, climate adaptations, political structure, family traditions, available technology and/or magic, laws, customs, casts and hierarchies, education, careers, and prevailing opinions on thousands of issues.

I'm Canadian. I do happen to like maple syrup and I don't mind hockey, but I prefer football. I use Canadian lingo like "eh", "chesterfield", and "toque". I'm polite. I'm a social-democrat. But I'm more than that.

I'm Catholic so I attend church on Sundays and celebrate Christian holidays. My grandmother was Dutch and grew up in a bakery, so we have many tasty treats that are traditional for her. We also celebrate St. Nicholas' Day in the traditional Dutch manner. I was a teenager at the turn of the millennium, so my vampires wear leather pants and listen to goth-metal, they do not sparkle, and I like my music to have good solid lyrics and a rough edge.

My religion, where my family originally hails from, how my grandmother was raised, when I grew up and developed my own tastes in pop-culture, all have an affect on me. So, while I belong to a large, overarching culture, the individual culture within my home and family is much more complex.

The following sections are designed to help you consider the multiple facets of culture and how they change based on gender, age, or wealth, among other things.

Societal Age and Tech Levels

We're talking Bronze Age, Victorian, Post-Modern sort of thing here. How advanced are they? When building a culture, this is the best place to start because so many other things will depend on what you choose here. Now, that's not to say you can't mix and match things, but this is going to give you a semi-firm base on which to build and some general boundaries to work within.

- What technology do they have access to? Remember, technology isn't just smart phones and televisions, it's everything from the wheel to metal weapons to horse shoes.
- What metals do they have access to? What have they learned to do with them? What type of weapons do they use? For a lot of traditional fantasy, your weapons are some form of swords, axes, spears, etc. while in science fiction writers lean towards modern guns and laser or pulse weapons.
- How do they build their houses? How efficient is their heating/cooling system? What about stoves or fridges or freezers?
- How do they make their clothes?
- What is the level of their medical knowledge? Do they have doctors or hospitals?

- Do they have any magic assisting any of these technologies?

There are some places where you want to bend historic accuracy, if you're not writing historic fiction. Like potatoes. And coffee. And birth control. And bathrooms. There are common places where authors allow primitive, or semi-primitive cultures to progress quicker than is historically accurate – or use magic to give these areas a boost. Other common ones are healing and freezers, both of which are often magically aided.

If you're reaching into the future, consider that our technology advances faster the more advanced it becomes. Each new idea or invention makes it quicker and easier for us to step even further forward. Consider, also, the level of cataclysmic event that would be required to set us back ten, fifty, or a hundred years, technology-wise.

Not all societies and cultures advance at the same rates. Even on Earth we still have very primitive tribes living in relative seclusion in Africa and South America. As these societies interact with each other there are a few possible outcomes.

First, we have aided progression – or the sharing of technology, as with the Europeans and the Native Americans. There was a sharing of tools and information between them which changed the Native American way of life and allowed the settlers to survive.

Second, if they are meeting from across vast distances, disease will be a huge factor. Germs are localized in worlds where people are born, live, and die in the same little village. Until you have wide spread international travel the spread of disease can be deadly.

Third, if meetings turn violent, there are a few things that would give one population an advantage over the other. The biggest advantage goes to the side with the most advanced weapons and armour. Bows and arrows against Spanish soldiers in metal armour? I don't think the arrows will cut it, and history says it didn't. A population has an advantage if the fight is on their territory. They know the terrain better, have better access to resources, and may have allies close at hand. I'm thinking Vietnam here. Which brings us to numbers. Don't underestimate the value of having more soldiers or fighters to throw at an enemy. The leaders' knowledge of warfare tactics will also come into the mix, as will the willingness of the people to fight for their leader, and the amount of training the common person has. Generally, though, the more advanced nation is most likely to win, unless you have a solid reason for them to lose, or some magical or divine intervention to toss in. And believe me, this fact has thrown a wrench in a story I was writing. I thought it was nearly done, now I'll be going back and rewriting large pieces of it.

I want to pause here and touch on utopias and dystopias. Generally, these are futuristic societal "ages" or "states of being" but you can write them in fantasies too. And you could turn a few historical eras into dystopias if you told them from the right point of view.

The utopia is the perfect world, with peace, prosperity, and plenty for all. No one goes hungry, there is no war, crime is minimalized, disease is all but eradicated. Conflict makes for good story telling, but where do you find conflict in the perfect world? The first place is a threat from outside. This could be between nations (one country exists in a Utopian state and is attacked by a neighbour), or between planets. The second source of conflict is from within.

Often in fiction Utopias are bought with the rights and freedoms of the people. Most Utopias have strict laws and a lot of governmental control. So long as the government is just and fair, and these missing freedoms don't cut away anything too precious, no one cares. But when leaders grow corrupt or power hungry, when more freedoms are taken, or are taken for the wrong reasons, the Utopia becomes a dictatorship with a pretty façade. Or, perhaps it was never a true Utopia, perhaps the government was lying all along, and people are getting suspicious. When that happens, dissent builds from within.

Utopias are hard to write and can lead to plot holes. You need to think long and hard about how your world/country manages to live in this state of peace and plenty. How do they prevent corruption? How do they prevent religions or cultures within their borders from disagreeing with each other? More importantly, how do they keep these disagreements from breeding distrust or violence? How do they keep everyone healthy and happy? How do they prevent class stratification or the hoarding of wealth? How do they adapt to outside influences and new inventions?

While Utopias have plenty and peace, Dystopias tend to have poverty and violence. The "mobs" are kept in check by armed government forces. The elite live in splendor, openly or secretly, and the rest live in squalor – and this is where Dystopias break for me. We learned this during the French revolution. Living in splendor in full view of starving people is a good way to get lynched no matter how good your security is. A smart Dystopian dictator would hide his wealth and insist that anyone else in the elite do the same. If everyone is suffering then the leader isn't a bad guy, they're just 'one of us poor suffering folk'.

Dystopias also rely on scapegoats – whose fault is it that things are bad? (A specific culture, an outside influence, a past event) And whose fault is it that things aren't getting better? Because people will ask those questions, and they'll expect answers.

While Utopias tend to be shiny and clean, Dystopias are either dirty, gritty, and dangerous or sterile and bland, over-controlled spaces where individuality and creativity cannot flourish. Utopias show us the best we can be, what we can strive for, while Dystopias serve as a warning against monetary greed, abuse of power, war, unchecked climate change, or whatever world issues the writer chooses to tackle.

Dystopias are excellent settings for revolutions and rebellions, for small groups of disenfranchised people to make big changes to their world. They are excellent also for the survival tale – post-apocalyptic or zombie-filled wastelands where small bands of survivors struggle to live and rebuild while fighting whatever threats come their way.

Utopias, on the other hand, do have a use, with their absence of internal struggle and their stable political climate. They are excellent backdrops for exploration stories, like Star Trek. When we no longer have to watch our backs against our neighbours we can turn our sights to loftier pursuits.

Class and Caste Structure

Class and Caste refer to a social hierarchy. Generally, class is fluid and based on a combination of social status, birth, wealth, marriage, and gender. Caste is more rigid and is simply a matter of birth.

If you're interested in a Caste system, look at ancient Indian customs. In India the Caste system dictated the type of job you could hold, (the lowest Caste which is considered unclean, does jobs like slaughtering animals and cleaning bathrooms while the highest Caste can become priests and leaders) who you could marry, and how you were treated in society. If you married wrong, you could drop down a Caste, but you could not climb the Caste ladder by making enough money or getting a better education.

Class is much more common and what most of us think of when we talk about social hierarchy. There are several variations of this and all can exist in the same society.

First, there is political hierarchy. In a monarchy it would look something like this (keeping in mind that different tiers may exist or not depending on the era):

King
Queen
Crown Prince
Princes and Princesses

Royals
Nobles
Wealthy People (landed gentry)
Trades People (poor people with talents)
Poor People (labourers)

In a theocracy it would look like this:
High Priest
Religious Council
Priests
Wealthy Laypeople
Everyone else

In a democracy it would look like this:
Chief elected official
Elected ruling councils of various levels
Legal voters
Those who will someday be able to vote (minors)
Those who are not legally allowed to vote

Generally, there is only one political structure in a country, but it's not the only hierarchy. There is also a religious hierarchy in places that do not have a theocracy. This hierarchy is limited to those who have jobs within the church/religious institution.

High Priest
Council of elders or advisors

Priests
Deacons
Students or Acolytes
Lay people

There may be some variation if there are two orders (one for men, one for women, for example) or if there are oracles or prophets involved.

If there is a complete separation of church and state, then everyone on this list falls under either wealthy/trades/poor people or under voters/non-voters at the "bottom" of the political hierarchies. In places where there is no theocracy but there is still an official religion and that religious group still holds some political sway the High Priest may hold a position on or equal to a ruling or advisory council, or equal to royals or nobles. From there the church hierarchy is shuffled into the political hierarchy.

There is no right or wrong choice here. Democracy, oligarchy, monarchy, theocracy, republic – there are examples of good ones and bad ones throughout history. Each has its benefits and pitfalls, and each is dependent on the moral compass of the people in charge.

If that wasn't complicated enough, there is also an economic hierarchy (again, things like the "Middle Class" didn't exist until the Industrial Revolution):

Old money – very wealthy
New money – very wealthy
Old money – lost some, or all, of its wealth but still has connections, or 'lower branches' of wealthy families.
Rich, businessmen, celebrities, etc.
Upper middle class (educated, skilled trades, doctors, lawyers, professionals, businessmen)
Middle class (trades, some education required)
Lower middle class (retail, service industry)
Lower class (working poor)
Impoverished, peasant, or enslaved

It's fairly easy to see how this hierarchy fits into any of the standard political hierarchies. Old money tends to be the Royals and Nobles. In a democracy the first seven or eight tiers fit into "legal voters" (or all of them if there is no slavery or voting restrictions).

And, to make matters more complicated, social hierarchies tend to be smaller (fewer tiers) earlier in history and larger (more tiers) after key historical events, like industrialization. If you are writing historical fiction, pay close attention to the class system of the era, and how people thought of themselves. In Europe the Middle Class as we know it today didn't exist until the Industrial Revolution.

Culture/clan/country of birth can play a role in where a person fits into any of these hierarchies. So can gender, religion, or sexuality.

Once you have established your various hierarchies it's time to decide how this will affect your culture.

- What separates the classes? How much interaction is there between classes?
- Rigidity/Mobility: how does someone move up or down the ladder?
- What are the privileges or responsibilities of each class?
- How are gender roles defined at each level? Is this a patriarchy, matriarchy, or egalitarian society?
- How concerned are they with bloodlines and last names?
    - Matrilineal/patrilineal or a blend? (which family tree do they follow)
    - Matrinomial/patrimonial? (whose last name is taken after marriage?)
- What is the status of bastards within the culture?
- How a person's rank or class changes how they interact with or view:
    - Law enforcement: do rich people get off with a warning more often?
    - Religious customs
    - Education

- General Social Etiquette: aristocrat manners versus "slumming it" with commoners
- Fashion: styles, availability
- Language/Slang
- Access to resources and weapons
- Acceptance of non-binary identities
- Virginity, pre-marital sex, rape

Look at our own world and the myriad of cultures in it, at different points in history, for ideas. Sometimes it is the wealthy who have to deal with more rules (like arranged marriages) and sometimes it is the commoners who have more rules (travelling restrictions, crippling debt, etc.).

In any society there's also the matter of power between genders. You have three choices here: a patriarchy (the greater power and privilege falls to the males), matriarchy (the greater power and privilege falls to the females), or egalitarian (power and privilege is granted with little or no regard to gender).

Most common in our world is the patriarchy, and there are issues that go along with that, issues we're still dealing with today as we attempt to reach an more egalitarian state. What women can do will be highly controlled. Often, they cannot vote, marry for love, hold a position in government, exert any "unnatural" control over their reproductive system, ask for a divorce, attend school, hold certain jobs, own land, inherit titles, property, or more than a certain amount of wealth, and so on. On the flip side they are expected to maintain a standard of beauty (especially in upper classes), keep the house, cook meals, raise the children, entertain guests, help with the gardens, etc.

One of the pitfalls of writing a Matriarchy is to either do a complete flip, making the men face the exact issues women face under the patriarchy (which doesn't always make sense given a difference in biology), or to make it a utopia where everyone is happy with the social order. If any one group of people has more power than another, if any one group of people has their rights, education, or job options limited by a group in power, there will be dissent. People will want to go down the path that is forbidden to them. They will want to wear what they are restricted from wearing. They will want to be with who they love instead of who their parents tell them to be with.

Instead of doing a complete flip, consider that it's not the job that's the problem but the attitude people take towards the job. In a patriarchy raising children is seen as less important that providing the food for the family (either as the money-earner or the hunter). Instead of making the men in a matriarchy raise the children, make raising children more important than hunting.

Also, a matriarchy is really no better than a patriarchy, and a patriarchy is no better than a matriarchy. Having them fight for power is fine, so long as it's obvious that there are flaws in both of them, and that no matter who wins, someone will lose. Having a broken matriarchy and then bringing in males to fix it and make it a working patriarchy isn't just bad story telling, it's reinforcing stereotypes and clichés that social advocates have been trying to squelch for decades. And we already know that a patriarchy isn't "better" for women in any way, shape, or form.

Religion

For our purposes, religion is any system of moral, ethical, or philosophical instruction that either worships or reveres one or more divine or enlightened beings. It's a very loose definition but covers everything from polytheism to monotheism to things like Buddhism which doesn't have a deity, just a man who "figured stuff out" and wanted to teach others.

In the previous section we discussed church hierarchy. Once you know that and how the church fits into your political spectrum there are a few things you need to consider:

- Regularity of church services: how often are they held? How often is it mandatory for people to attend? Is there a cost to attend? Is it a requirement or a privilege? How ritualized is the service?
- Holy Book: Is there one? Is there more than one? Is this a strictly oral tradition? If you have a book, who has access to it?
- Buildings: how formal is the physical building of the church? What is this building called? If there is no official building, where do they worship?
- Feast days, festivals, holy days, church calendar
- Formality of priesthood and how much education is required to join

- Gender of priesthood: male, female, or both? Or do they have separate roles (like priests and nuns in the Catholic church)?
- Level of involvement in politics
- Wedding or equivalent tradition, and religious opinions on pre-marital sex and divorce
- Birth/naming traditions, religious opinions on bastards and/or single mothers
- Terms for buildings (church, temple, chapel), officials (priests, deacons, rabbi, teacher, holy man, etc.), rituals, etc.
- Is joining the church as a priest a respected profession, or a place to drop embarrassing offspring?
- What are death or funeral rituals like? What is done with the bodies and why? Does this differ based on gender or class? What are the rituals surrounding grief or mourning?
- What is this religion's official stance on:
    - Magic/Science
    - Gender roles
    - Non-binary identities
    - Class/Caste, charity, alms
    - Race/Species, racism
    - Royalty/Politics
    - Virginity, sex, and rape

Religion can be difficult to write on because of our own religious bias. If you as a writer believe religions here on Earth are fake, that there are no gods, that religious people made it all up thousands of years ago, then you may find it easier to write about societies where this is also true.

If you follow a religion there is the temptation to model the virtuous, perfect, true religion in your story on the religion you follow.

Just remember, people who believe in a religion believe it is real, that there really is a divine something there, and that their religion is the true religion, or at least it is a valid religion. Only people outside a religion, or disenfranchised believers, ever consider a religion to be false or made up. Your characters will be living in their religion and will believe it, unless of course it's part of the plot or their character to be a doubter.

Whether you believe in god or not there are a lot of good fantasy novels out there that imagine pantheons of gods who are very real and who show up in the books and do powerful feats of magic and work miracles and give orders. No matter your beliefs you should feel free to explore all forms of religious practice, and the possibility that the gods are either real and involved, real and absent, or made up – whatever suits your story.

Religion in science-fiction is a strange thing. The majority of writers seem to view the future as religion free, and yet, I witnessed a Klingon wedding on Star

Trek: Deep Space Nine. Religion will not cease, not for humans, not for aliens. Yes, there are atheists among humans, and there will be atheists among aliens, but being a scientist does not mean you can't believe in a higher power. And just because you are showing a unified utopian future (like Star Trek) doesn't mean people have to give up their religions. Instead of a world where everyone figures out religion is bad and stops believing, write a world where everyone figures out how to believe in different things without fighting each other.

Religious beliefs are a powerful thing and can motivate a character to great feats of charity, compassion, or self-sacrifice. They open doors to self-doubt, to crisis of faith, and to other inner conflicts that can make your character development more interesting. The grieving process takes on an added dimension when you must grapple with your faith (what kind of god allows a person to die so horribly anyways?). Religious conflicts don't have to be between religions, or between sects of a religion, they can be inner, personal struggles as well.

Yes, atheists can be just a moral and upstanding as a believer and yes, a religious person can do just as many horrible, amoral things as anyone else. So feel free to include religion, as a truth or as a cultural construct, as a part of character development, or a part of the larger plot struggle, in any era, past or future.

Political and Legal Systems

You should already have a political system selected (monarchy, theocracy, democracy, oligarchy, hybrid) and a political hierarchy outlined. Now it's a matter of figuring out how that political system works, day-to-day, through the legal system.

There are several branches of the political/legal system: administrative, criminal, personal harm, taxation, and so on.

- Who helps the ruling class with day-to-day tasks? Who spreads the word when a decision is made? Who needs to know? Who enforces it?
- Taxes – who pays whom, for what, on what, how much, and when? Is this a money only system, or can taxes be paid in goods and services?
- How formal is the legal system? Are their courts? Lawyers and judges? Police?
- Who makes the laws?
- Does the gender/class/non-binary identity of the victim impact the enforcement of a law?
- Property and possession laws:
    o Who can own property (land, houses)
    o Who can own businesses
    o Inheritance of money, property, and titles
    o Vandalism and theft

- Property upkeep
- Loan protections
- Trade regulations
- Possession of weapons or other "sensitive" items
- Bodily Harm Laws
  - Murder
  - Physical assault
  - Sexual crimes: harassment, assault, rape
  - Does the identity or class of the victim or the accused change how the case is handled
- Speech Laws
  - Verbal Harassment
  - Slander, liable
  - Hate speech
- Treason – what constitutes treason? Who oversees the trial?
- Religious involvement in legal proceedings
  - Divorce
  - Claiming a bastard
  - Crimes against the church (failure to uphold a religious obligation, theft from the church) – who oversees the trial? What punishments are they allowed to enact?
- Magical implications on law
  - Using magic to break the law
  - Using magic to uphold the law
  - Truth Sayers, truth spells, truth potions

- Is there corruption within the law enforcement? At what level? Who is aware? How wide spread?

There are two view points to "the law" – the way it should work (justice is blind) and the way it does work (often marginalized groups are not given equal treatment under the law, or stereotypes come into play). Be honest with yourself and your characters. This divide is sadly normal. Feel free to create the ideal that your world is supposed to live, and the reality it is living. It will build tension and allow young, naive characters to come up against difficult situations. Also, feel free to throw in some utopian ideals, and let your characters live them. We need more uplifting fiction.

When writing historical fiction, or any fiction really, keep in mind that we are products of our time and that social change happens slowly. Women in the Middle Ages did not think about inequality, class, patriarchy, or racism the same way women today think about it. Most of your characters will fit the social mold of their time.

There were always rebels. Elizabeth Barrett Browning wrote two poems titled "To George Sand: A Desire" and "To George Sand: A Recognition" – George Sand was a woman in the Victorian era who got in trouble for wearing pants and took on a man's name. There are many stories of men being arrested for sleeping with other men. Jane Austen made a career out of writing novels that critiqued the landed gentry of Britain and their social habits.

More recently were the hippies who lived in a way that bucked multiple conventions (birth control and pre-marital sex, recreational drugs, passivism, alternative religions). Plus, the Civil Rights movement, the Suffragettes, modern feminism, and the LBGTQ+ equality movement.

But, traditionally a person, even a slave, will not rebel unless they are shown that there is another way to live. Women who see only one way that society works believe this is the only way society works. When a few of those women witness another culture, with other ideas about women, and start talking then minds start changing and movements are born.

It takes quite a few people saying "hold on a minute, this doesn't make sense" before a movement is born. And those first people will generally say these things only to a trusted few, under their breath, in secret. Because if their ideas are not well received it could mean death or torture. Look at Les Miserable – their revolution failed because people were too afraid to stand with them. Things just weren't bad enough to rally the mob to their side. Most people in their life will tell them to be quiet, don't attract attention, don't rock the boat, because it's safer.

Religious views and legal views on matters can differ wildly. It's legal in Canada to get married no matter the gender of each party but that doesn't mean all the religious agree with it. Differences between religious law and state law can build tension in your society, as it clearly does in our own.

If your story is about political change, you need to dedicate enough time to the build up, or reference that the build up has been happening. You also need to include a lot of people, even people your fledgling movement will benefit, who stand against it and try to discourage your rebels from stirring up trouble.

If you're already in the middle of a rebellion you owe your reader some explanation of how you got there.

Job/Education

This is an example both of how your base societal level can determine cultural attributes, and how you can progress an aspect of a culture beyond, or hold it back from, a specific historical point.

- Formality of education: are children taught at home by their mothers or do they attend a school?
- Duration of formal education: when do they start? When are they finished?
- Topics covered in formal education: math, literacy, history, etc.
- Topics covered in the home: hunting, cleaning animals, cooking, cleaning, knitting, sewing, checking the oil in a car, changing a car tire, feeding animals – these are often seen as essential life skills and will change depending on the time period.
- Differences by class/parentage: do nobles get more education than peasants?
- Differences by profession: what specialized topics need to be covered to learn a profession? Which professions have apprenticeships? Which professions require more education than others?
- Differences by gender: is one gender's education considered more important? Is there a difference in topics covered? Are they educated together in apart?

- Culture/Species – what are they taught about other cultures or species in their world? If the lived in a mixed/mingled region does someone's culture/species change how much education they get?

Once your character has an education they need a job. Which job they take and why depends partly on your character and partly on your culture.

Looking at historic novels, or historically inspired fantasy (period fantasy), you'll see a lot of apprenticeships taking place, often with at least one of the sons taking on the same job as their father. Other sons will apprentice where they are needed in the community. The size of their village/city will determine how many black smiths, carpenters, and healers are needed at any given time. Of course, 'historic' events, like a war, can increase the need for specific jobs (like soldiers, smiths, and healers).

In more modern times, like now, we choose a job based on what we want to do, what we're good at, what will pay us well, or sometimes what our parents want for us. It's not often that we follow in our parents' footsteps anymore. There is a movement back towards apprenticeships in many professions, especially the hands-on ones like mechanics.

Often, jobs are stratified by class. It's still hard for poor people to become doctors or lawyers because of the cost of school. It doesn't matter what era your story is set in or based on, some jobs will be for higher class people, and others will be for lower class people. Your society will have opinions on different types of jobs (see them as dirty, frivolous, simple, requiring talent, etc.) and on the people who do them.

Something else I learned in writing this book, is that "black smith" is not, in fact, a catch all phrase for 'someone who makes stuff out of metal'. An armourer makes armor, specifically plate mail, but also chain mail and other forms of metal armor. A blade smith, sword smith, or Master at Arms, is the person who makes weapons for a lord's retinue of guards or army. A farrier makes horse shoes and puts them on horses. I smith or metal smith makes tools, dishes, and other basic metal items. A blacksmith works specifically with iron.

Now, in a small town, your farrier may also be your smith. When an army is travelling the Master at Arms might also make on-the-go repairs to armor. And, if you're creating your own culture, you make not have these specific differences.

If there are this many difference between types of smiths, think of the specialization in the medical field, in engineering and mechanics, or even in law, in today's society. Imagine how much more specialized some of these jobs will become as we develop space travel. An engine mechanic working on shipping drones will not be qualified to work in a starship engine room. The guy responsible for keeping the city busses on schedule and on their correct routes will not be hired on as an interplanetary navigations officer (unless of course he only took the job with the city while waiting for his dream job on a starship to open up).

Interaction Between Species/Cultures

Just look at our world now. Racial and religious tensions are some of the biggest threats in our political spheres, world wide. We have a long history of hating people for the gods they worship, the country they were born in, or the colour of their skin. Your fictional world doesn't have to follow our history, but differences are a natural cause of tension. We all want our way to be the right way and seeing a different way of doing things can make it easy to feel invalidated. How your characters react to different people will tell a lot about them and their culture.

- Racial Tensions: between members of the same species but from different countries. Perhaps they have different skin tones, different languages, or different religions.
- Inter-species Tensions: between members of different sentient species, whether alien or fantastical.
- How do these opinions differ by gender, either of the perceiver or the perceived?
- Does opinion differ by regions (those living closer to a different species/culture may feel differently about them than those living far away)? Familiarity does not always lead to acceptance – those closest to "those people" may resent them the most.

- Inter-racial or inter-species children: what is their status? Between which species can there be children (humans and elves but not humans and trolls, for example)

    While skin colour, religion, etc. are often used as excuses for hatred and war, there are often underlying causes – mostly the struggle for power over resources and space. Your leaders may want the gold in them-there hills, but the common man may not be willing to risk his life to line someone else's pockets with gold. Telling him that "those people" are evil or dangerous is far more effective in rousing the masses to fight.

    When writing about these interactions be aware of the culture propaganda, and the ulterior motives of the ruling class.

Magic and/or Technology Usage

Technology includes everything from smart phones to space ships to toilets to freezers to shovels. At some point in history even the most mundane, basic, outdated tool you use was a cutting-edge innovation. Someone invented it, someone else improved it, and at some point, it became so common place we stopped thinking about it.

Generally new technology is only available to select groups of people, such as people who work in specific fields or the wealthy. Take microscopes for example. Only doctors and scientists working in the best equipped labs had access to them. At some point universities would have gotten a hold of them for their labs as well. Then trade schools, high schools, and eventually you could buy them for your kids for Christmas. Sure, there was a wide array of type and quality available, but they became common place.

That is an example of career or trade specific technology. Any modern convenience is an example of wealth-first technology. Machines that wash your clothes? Running water in your house? Electric lights? A freezer that doesn't need a fresh block of ice every two days? All these things were available only to people who could afford them. As they became easier to make the price came down and more people could buy them. Then a better version would come out. Now more people could afford the old version but only the wealthy could invest in the newer, better, version. Most recently we went through this with internet, home computers, cellphones, and smart phones.

Deciding what technology your society has access to in general is a good place to start. Figuring out who in the society has access to what and at what cost makes your culture a living breathing thing.

Weapons is a big one. Even today governments try to limit who has access to which types of weapons and under which conditions. In the days of knights in shining armor it took a lot of money to be more than a common foot soldier. You had to provide your own armor and plate mail was expensive. If you wore plate you needed a large horse to carry you and all that metal. You probably needed a squire to help you get in and out of it and carry your supplies, and they would require a horse or pony as well – and all four of you required food and lodgings. Plus, weapons for you. And upkeep on the weapons, armor, and horses.

Generally, commoners were only allowed weapons that could be passed off as tools. A knife for cleaning their game, a pitchfork could double as a weapon, but not a spear unless they were part of a local militia and certainly not a sword unless someone in their family was a soldier at some point. Armed commoners were dangerous and harder to keep downtrodden. And metal weapons were expensive to buy and maintain.

Access to technology will change as technology evolves and evolve it will. You cannot stop progress.

One of my pet-peeves is stories with long lived species where nothing ever changes. How much faster do you think medicine, science, and technology would evolve if the research didn't have to change hands every twenty to fifty years? If one person or one team could continue to build off their own theories and ideas for a hundred years, or a thousand, without the learning curve of someone else picking up where they left off, wouldn't things progress faster, not slower? There are reasons why this might not hold true – like a culture using magic instead of technology so they never develop the technology for that task.

I want to quickly mention two examples that I do not own or have any rights to, one that I feel does this well, and one that I feel did this poorly.

First, Avatar, the television shows, The Last Airbender and its sequel, The Legend of Korra, handled this well. Within the first series you saw the Fire Nation evolve from supporting the balance of the four nations, to reckless war mongers, back to supporting the balance. You saw the North and South water tribes evolve away from each other, with the South becoming more lenient and egalitarian much earlier than the North.

There was an obvious technological jump between the first series and the second, moving from a late feudal era to early 1900s with motor vehicles in urban centers, better police forces and law enforcement, and even radios. The beginning of season two hinges on the struggle between tradition and progress.

Second, the Dark Jewels books by Anne Bishop. She has a combination of long and short-lived humans and within each group some of the population is blessed with magical abilities while most are not. The prologue of the original series starts hundreds of years before the main storyline and yet nothing changes.

Now, the Blood use magic for damn near everything so they don't need to develop the technology for things like medicine or food preservation. But over two-thirds of the population can't do magic. They rely on old methods (like ice boxes) or paying someone with magic to do things for them.

There are wealthy non-magic people in their world, people who have good educations. Why have none of them figured out electricity in the thousands of years this society has existed? What about coal or steam powered transportation so they don't have to rely on overpriced access to the magical transportation system? The society remains frozen in place with no technological development for thousands of years. The oldest named character is over ten thousand years old, and the world of his first lifespan looks no different from the world of the main story line.

A lot has changed in the last five thousand years in our world. A lot should change in any world in five thousand years. So, unless your magical population is violently suppressing scientific study in the non-magical population they are going to discover steam power, electricity, or some equivalent thereof.

That being said, I'm a huge fan of both Avatar and the Dark Jewels and revisit both worlds often.

Different cultures within your world may have access to different technology and may share their technology among their citizens differently. This brings up the issue of trade.

There are many examples in the ancient world of trade secrets. One group of people figures out how to make glass and they don't teach outsiders how to make it. Or they breed the best horses or grow a certain type of crop and guard the seeds. By guarding their resources or processes in this way they forced other people to trade with them. "Sell a man a fish, he has to buy one from you again tomorrow, and the next day, and the next day. Teach a man to fish and he'll catch his own damn dinner, and no one will pay you to do it anymore." That is how the saying goes, right?

What does group A have that group B wants and vice versa? Could be food, could be textiles, could be raw resources, could be other goods. Trade can be done for economic reasons, but also for political ones. Making a one-time gift of something rare, like a prize horse or hunting dog, can cement allegiances between countries.

Now consider this: what does group A have that they don't want to share? If you've successfully invented a catapult you don't want to sell the finished product, or the plans, to your neighbours just in case they decide to invade you. Generally, blueprints, plans, and processes fall under this. You may be willing to sell glass but not the secret to making it. You may sell your crops, but not the seeds to grow it. And of course, specialized tools, weapons, or animal breeds often fell into this category as well.

Magic is technology or abilities that run on make believe instead of on science. If you went back and time and showed someone a steam engine or airplane they'd think it was sorcery of the highest order because they wouldn't be able to understand the science behind it. We believed the sun rose and set at the whim of the gods and that rainbows were magic bridges.

You may end up creating a world where magic is just an incomplete understanding of the natural world, like ours You may create a world where "real magic" exists.

Your system of magic will need certain boundaries and guidelines, or it will break your story. These boundaries include who can do what, what the magic is capable of, the cost of doing magic, the process of doing magic, and the process of learning magic.

Who can do what? Is magic a skill that anyone can learn if they have the proper tools and teachers? Is the ability to learn magic limited to a certain group? Can different people do/learn different types of magic within a single world?

When considering these questions consider what the division or boundary is. In Harry Potter and in The Dark Jewels magic is innate in specific people and that ability is inherited – a genetic trait as it were. BUT people who can do magic still need to be taught to control their magic. Perhaps your magic is cultural – elves can do it, but humans can't. Or gender based (be wary of this, there are major pitfalls to this style of magic). Maybe humans can make magical potions while elves can cast spells, or men's magic comes from water while women's magic comes from earth.

In Avatar the magic is elemental, it is control over and usage of fire, earth, water, or wind. If you can use one of those four things to do something, like using wind to slam a door or water to knock a person over, you can do it with magic. In Harry Potter there seems to be very few limits to what magic can do – if you know the right spell or potion.

What is the magic capable of? This includes, how a person's individual talent changes what they can do, as well. Most obviously, magic gets used for combat – fire balls, lightning bolts, ice spikes, calling up storms and earthquakes to halt armies, invisibility spells and teleportation to aid assassins. Equal to that is healing. But what else is magic used for? Lighting candles from across the room or summoning floating balls of light? Enchanting some object to deliver messages? Can people store and carry things in non-physical magical "bags"? Can they make clutter around their house invisible when guests arrive? Or talk to animals? Or have a magical pen that writes down what they're saying or thinking?

That brings us to: what is the cost of doing magic? What is the process of doing magic? And what is the source of the magic?

The source may be innate ability, but it may also be charms, rituals, incantations, spiritual or divine in origin, potions, or spells. It may be like The Force, an energy that certain people can tap into. Doubling back to ability, some people may be able to grab more of that energy, or use it more skillfully than others, either through training or raw talent.

On Supernatural, anyone with the knowledge of specific rituals or spells can use them. They don't need any special ability or talent or genetics. But they need to know the ritual and perform it perfectly or it won't work, at best, or will backfire in some painful way, at worst. This is the process of doing magic. What spell or magic word needs to be recited? What runes do you need to draw? What ingredients have to go in the pot? What arm motions do you need to do?

With complicated spells there's always the risk of being interrupted. Is a spell caster vulnerable while they are casting? Are there consequences to being interrupted? If so they may require an ally to guard their back during this time.

Finally, there is the cost of doing magic. In video games this is your manna or magic or whatever. It's a little bar at the bottom and when it's empty you can't cast anymore spells. Each spell costs a certain number of spell points. Does your magic require a certain amount of focus or energy on the part of the caster? Does it drain them in some way or take time to recharge? Are they vulnerable in any way, other than being without magic, during this recharge time?

Generally, the faster the process the higher the cost or longer the recharge time. The slower or more involved the process the lower the cost or slower the recharge time. We design magic this way to avoid overpowered systems or characters.

So, you know who can do magic, what that magic can do, what it costs the character to perform it, and the process they must complete to perform it. But how did they learn to do it?

Even with innate abilities, like bending in Avatar, or like the elemental abilities on Zoedar, some degree of training is required to learn, first, to control it, and second, to use it to its full potential. With spells, like in Harry Potter, or the Great Lady's Magics on Zoedar, the caster must learn the proper words and motions required to cast the spell, and then they must memorize them as well or be forced to carry around a book, or notes.

Who is in charge of this training? Is this part of the formal education system? Your answer to these questions will depend greatly on your answers in other sections regarding how the ruling class, general population, and religious leaders view magic.

The Catholic Church viewed witchcraft as evil while the Pagans just saw it as another form or worship, another ability. Is magic outlawed in your world? Or secret? If so how does your magical character find a teacher?

The 'Unimportant' Stuff

We get so caught up in governments and magical systems, in schools and churches, in laws and trade, that we might overlook the important 'unimportant' stuff that makes up a culture. Music, dance, theatre, storytelling, celebratory traditions, and food. Just try to describe any culture on Earth without mentioning any of those things.

Music: class and caste are going to play a roll in what instruments a character has access to and how formal their lessons will be. The wealthy boy will have a violin, brand new, shipped from a master craftsman in a large city. He will have regular lessons with a tutor and will learn to play the measured pieces of the upper class. The poor boy will have a battered fiddle that's been in the family four generations. He will learn from his father and grandfather and the rest he will learn by trial and error. He will play jigs and folk songs.

The wealthy will play clarinets and oboes, the poor will play penny whistles and reed flutes. The poor will have hand drums and cow bells, the wealthy will have timpani or kettle drums. Time period will also play a role in which classes have access to what type of instrument.

Dance: There are so many traditions of dance, from ballroom dancing we know now to the court dances of bygone days, from ballet to jazz to whatever people are doing in nightclubs these days. Traditionally the wealthy had stricter dances with choreographed steps while the peasant class had looser 'rules' on their dances (though I've seen some pretty complex jigs). Also, the newer a type of music or dance, the looser the rules will be. The longer people have been doing it, the more traditional and "regulated" the steps and style will be. Religion can play a role in the style of dance as well. Cultures with conservative religious views towards sex, or with strict rules regarding the interaction of genders, will have stricter rules regarding what is acceptable in dance as well.

Theatre: There was a time when acting was a 'dirty' profession. Consider how your actors are treated – as poor vagabonds, wanderers, and potential thieves, or as celebrities with an amazing talent. Is there a difference between the stages and opera houses of the big cities and the community theatres of the small towns? Theatre leads directly into movies, depending on the tech level of your society, and the same questions apply. As well, was it seen as a fun afternoon out to go to the theatre, or a waste of time and money?

Storytelling: Myths and legends, generational stories, these are the life blood of a culture. How do the myths of the common people compliment or contradict the formal religion of the land? If the common person is illiterate and has no access to the Holy Book, what stories do they learn? Where do they learn it from? How accurate or fluid is your culture's oral tradition?

If you have a written tradition, what is the place of fiction in your society? Is it fluff to fill the lazy afternoons of the upper-class woman? Are writers seen as important talented people? Or as layabouts? Who has access to historical texts? Or religious ones? Are books copied by hand or do you have a printing press? Or do scholars keep fairies tho do all the copying?

Traditions: They can be cultural traditions, like putting your shoe out for St. Nicholas Day, a tradition upheld by most of a country for dozens, if not hundreds, of years. They can be family traditions, like when you put up your Christmas tree, or who makes breakfast on Christmas morning.

Traditions give us a sense of continuity. The Christmas morning breakfast I feed my kids is very similar to the one I ate as a child (and consists of orange juice, candy canes, chocolate, bacon, and either cinnamon buns or croissants). Tradition connects us to parents and grandparents, and to neighbours. Traditions provide a powerful sense of belonging and unity, one that can strengthen a family or a nation.

Food: what are the favourite recipes? Perogies are distinctly Ukrainian, scotch is a drink for upper class men in smoking rooms, tea is British, bannock is Native American. Regional access to types of food, plus a unique way of preparing it, creates cultural or family food traditions. As well, people who travel for a living, like sailors and traders, or nomadic cultures, will have a very different diet from stationary people, especially in pre-car, pre-refrigerator societies.

If you have a character visiting a new region for the first time they may be surprised by how spicy the stew is, or that they have ale instead of wine.

These little bits of culture may not be important in the big scheme of the plot, but they are important to building your characters. They can also play a big role in bringing people together. Food, music, and celebration is a great way to bridge political or religious differences.

Another thing to consider are the menial jobs: garbage disposal, waste disposal, and everything connected to them.

What do people do with their garbage? Composting was a big part of life until the industrial revolution and is still a big part of life in rural areas today. But you don't compost meat or bone – that has to be fed to the dogs or burned or tossed out with the trash. Do people burn their own garbage? How much garbage do they produce?

What do bathrooms look like? If there is no plumbing system, no central waste treatment facility, where does the waste go? If they have outhouses, who empties them?

In Shakespearean times chamber maids dumped the contents of their lady's chamber pot out the window so it would join the rain water and flow down to wherever the water went. (Hence the line in Romeo and

Juliet about "putting their women against the wall" – to show respect to a woman you allowed her to walk nearest the curb so that she wouldn't get splashed.) This Shakespeare reference is a perfect example of how and why a detail so tiny and so often omitted from world building can play into culture in a larger sense. Later customs changed and it was polite for the man to walk near the street to prevent the lady from being splashed by traffic. As technology (both transportation and sanitation) changed, so too did cultural norms around courting.

Waste management will also impact the cleanliness of your setting, and the prevalence of disease.

This is not something we want to talk about but I'm going to talk about it anyways. Periods. Sorry guys, it's a fact of life. If you have humans in your story, the females menstruate. If you have mammalian, humanoid species they likely menstruate as well.

What is the cultural view on women's periods? Do you have a culture that allows women a few days of peace to rest and meditate? Or do you have a culture that isolates women because they are ritually unclean? What are the cultural views on sex during that time? Does a girl's first period signify anything special? Is it a time to rejoice in her first steps towards womanhood? Or is it seen as a curse? This also ties into bathrooms and hygiene as women will need a way to deal with the blood flow and either clean or dispose of these hygiene products. This is second nature for most women, but it doesn't hurt to research how these things were handled in other historical eras. And for men, can I recommend that, should you choose to include something about menstruation in your story, that you have a woman read it over for you? This is one of those things where you'll end up looking foolish if you get it wrong.

I want to touch on death again here. I mentioned it briefly in the Religion section but it's important, not just in a ritual way, but in a health and sanitation way as well.

What is done with dead bodies? Cremation? Burial? How advanced are their embalming practices? Who handles the dead? A priest? A healer? The family?

What happens if there is a war? How quickly are battle fields cleared? Are there fantasy creatures that feast on the dead? Or just the usual crows and other carrion feeders? An entire field of dead bodies rotting in the sun is going to stink, and attract pests, and breed bugs and rats. The rotten meat can foul water supplies, the blood can destroy the fertility of the field.

In East Indian culture anyone who touches feces, or the dead are ritually unclean. These jobs are left to those of the lowest caste. How does your culture view waste management and dead bodies? How does your culture view those who handle these jobs?

History

Cultures change. As their technology changes, as they meet with other cultures, they take in new ideas and must change their old ones. Adopt, adapt, and modify – cultures that fail to change will fall.

If you're writing a one-off novel that takes place over the course of a few months to a few years this may not be important unless it's a key point in your plot. If you're planning a series that spans generations, or are planning multiple stand-alone novels in one universe, you're going to find this much more important.

How have all these things you've brainstormed changed over time?
How will they continue to evolve over time?
What historical influences affect change?
Who is resistant to this change? Who welcomes it?
Is this a slow change or a revolution?
How are the changes justified?

Keep in mind also, that "the winners write the history books". The truth of what happened may be lost, buried in myth, lack of public education, or propaganda. Different groups (the church and the Royal family for example) may have different views of history, and different opinions on the causes and outcomes.

The common people will rely on what the officials tell them. In past times this was because the officials controlled the flow of information almost completely by keeping the population illiterate. In science fiction you can make use of fake news, propaganda machines, falsified documents, records, or studies, and media black-outs to control the flow of information.

As your history progresses, keep in mind that living conditions always improve first for the wealthiest and trickle down very slowly to the poor. The introduction of electronic ovens and washing machines into North American culture is a prime example of this. What we now consider a basic necessity was once a luxury. There were still poor families in rural regions with hand wringer-washers after World War II. And sadly, even today, there are people without reliable sources of drinking water.

Example 1: The Alarans, Pt. 2

The Alarans live on one of the moons orbiting the planet where the Zoedavian Chronicles take place. They live in isolation from the other species and cultures. The moon is one-third water (a small ocean, a lake, and some rivers), one-third forest, and the final third is split between urban and agriculture.

Architecturally they are Roman inspired with clean lines, pillars, and cobble stone paved roads. Their fashion is like Roman or Greek as well.

Their government is a theocracy. The queen is also the high priestess. She is assisted by a council of high ranking Alarans who advice her on political matters and an oracle who advises her on religious matters. The oracle is attended by acolytes who take care of the temple.

Alarans worship Sadeah, the goddess of law and order, as their primary deity but honour all the deities in the global pantheon (there are nine total). Their ceremonies are structured and serious and attendance is required by law.

The queen is the top of the political and social hierarchy. She is also the judge in all legal cases. Beneath her is the council who also stand as the jury. Each council member is in charge or a group of Alarans based on their gifts.

The more general the Alaran's gift the higher up the hierarchy they are. The Angel of Elements is on the council, the Angels of Light, Dark, Energy, Fire, Earth, Water, and Wind are next. Beneath the Angel of Water is the Angel of Rain and so on. They have some magical abilities, or special talents, related to the gift they're born with.

Alarans are so long-lived as to be near-immortal. The only way to kill them is massive blood loss, decapitation, or the removal of their wings. They have very few children. They rarely die of old age.

Alarans are very open minded about sex – so long as everyone involved is fully consenting they don't care what you do or who you do it with. There is no stigma against single parents and no one is required to marry, not in order to engage in sexual activities and not in order to have children. Divorce is not common but there is also no stigma against it.

Alarans are racist. They do not like surface dwellers, except Phoenixes (who are believed but the surface dwellers to be myths). If an Alaran is born without wings, it's assumed that the child is half human or half elfish, so the child is put to death. There is a chance, in those cases, that the mother might be put to the death as well.

Their other crimes involve physical injury, theft, damage to property and such. Punishments may be physical in nature (whipping, for example) or may require reparations be made.

Their economy is trade-based. With such a small population they do not farm more than they need. They are more communal that capitalistic and take care of each other. That's not to say that there aren't grudges and feuds within their society, just that they are able to separate their personal feelings from their social duty.

Because they have so few children at a time in their society there is no formal education system. They are taught to read and write at home and are apprenticed to someone with a similar gift.

Example 2: An Underground Utopia

The Underground series is a near-future science fiction adventure for middle grade readers. Humans are the only species and their culture is fairly similar to the one we live in now (North America). Because they have moved to underground mega-cities there has been a shift away from capitalism towards a more socialist economic structure.

History: There was a war that quickly escalated to the use of nuclear weapons. Dozens, if not hundreds, of cities across North America were reduced to rubble in the span of days. Fortunately, these underground shelters had already been built and hundreds of thousands of people were escorted underground to safety. The rest were lost to the war that continues to rage on the surface three generations later. The surface is unlivable but underground people are safe.

Economy: The cities, called Complexes, have full shopping malls inside them with clothing stores, hobby stores, grocery stores, and drug stores. This requires retail workers and janitorial staff. As well, each Complex specializes in some sort of manufacturing or primary industry. Some have massive greenhouses, others make batteries or other parts for the large, automated vehicles on the surface (the ones still waging the war or transporting goods between Complexes). Some make clothing, others make cheese and butter, others make electronics. Goods are then transported to the other Complexes on automated transports.

Everyone lives lean and makes their clothes and electronics last as long as possible because so much is needed to maintain the war effort. At the same time, they have free access to gyms, arcades, swimming pools, bowling alleys, and other social services (which requires staff to work at each, plus doctors and other social service and medical service providers). There are churches and community centres and even unions.

Education and Living Conditions: Young couples start in small apartments with a single bedroom. When their first child is two, or when they have a second child, they are moved to a three-bedroom apartment. Here they will stay until both children move out and then they will return to a one-bedroom unit. The children begin school at five or six, depending on their birthdays and developmental progress.

They attend Kindergarten to Grade Five in the elementary wing of their district's school system, then move into a new wing for Grades Six to Eight. After Grade Eight there is a selection test and many of the fourteen-year-olds are shipped to other Complexes where their interests and talents will be of the most use. This also keeps the genetic pool fresh in each Complex.

Transfer students are sent in secure pods on the automated transports. They complete school, Grades Nine through Twelve and possibly some trade school or university instruction (there is a High School section and Post Secondary sections within their district), and then begin their careers. They live at home, or with a foster or boarding family, until they marry and then move into a single bedroom unit until they have kids.

Political and Legal: There is a security force that maintains order within the Complex. Their laws are similar to current laws, no theft, no vandalism, no assault, or any variation thereof. There are additional laws for public safety regarding access to the power plants and the warehouse.

There are district overseers who are in charge of getting supplies to the stores, the school districts, and the security forces. There is one overseer responsible for all the district overseers and it is his or her job to communicate with the other districts to coordinate transports and such. The military is separate from the governing of the Complexes.

Communication and Travel: Within a single Complex there are land lines and cellphones. Because of the radiation and the depth cellphones cannot call out to other Complexes, only landlines. They also have computers with internet, so they can communicate over video chat or by email between Complexes. This means siblings and friends separated by the transfers can keep in touch with each other.

There are two travel networks within the Complex: the lifts take people up and down and the transports take people between districts on a single level. The automated surface transports are the only way to move between Complexes and only one passenger transport goes out each year.

Characters

Names and Identifiers

What's in a name? Well, when you're writing a book, a lot. Names, nicknames, and titles, are some of the first things we generally find out about a character. This is a tag for the reader to remember them by. Because of this, it's important not to put in too many names that look or sound too similar to each other.

I know a Jonathan, three Johns, and a Jean-Claude. This is completely normal in our world. In fiction, it's just nicer to keep the repetitive names to a minimum. There are some very good examples of repetitive names done right, but there are lot more examples of this being done wrong. I stopped reading a book halfway through chapter one because the first two characters you meet had such similar names that I couldn't keep them straight!

Here are some things to think about when naming your characters:

- What is their first name? Why did their parents choose this name? Does this name mean anything?
- Do they have a middle name? What is it? Why did their parents choose it? Does it mean anything?

- Do they have a surname, family name, clan name, or other similar identifier? Does it have meaning?
- Do they have nicknames that are short forms of their names? (Jessica becomes Jess; Christopher becomes Chris or Topher) Do they have other nicknames? (Kiddo, Old Boy, Mouse) Who gave it to them? How did they earn it? Who calls them by their nickname? Who refuses to call them by anything but their full name? Do they like their nicknames?
- Do they have any titles of rank? (Captain, Lord, Lady, Master, Sir ...) Titles of accomplishment? (Vlad the Impaler)
- Does their name suit their species/country of birth/country of family origin/historic setting?

Some names didn't exist as names in some historic periods. I've included in the references at the end of this book a link to a blog edited by Dr. Sarah Uckelman about the history of names in Europe. If you're writing historic fiction this is something to be aware of.

Physical Appearance and Attributes

Appearance is the second big identifier for your reader to recognize your character. Having one blonde friend and one brunette friend makes it easy to tell them apart. Just keep in mind that there are a lot of clichés when it comes to physical appearances.

Blondes are not necessarily dumb or ditzy. Redheads don't always have a temper. Big guys aren't always slow or dumb, and neither are country kids. Not all black people are in gangs, not all gay men are overtly effeminate. These clichés are lazy short hands. You say, "Torri was a dumb blonde" and everyone knows her instantly. But, I say again, this is lazy storytelling. Give Torri black hair and a father with a doctorate and then show me all her clumsy dumb mistakes. Your readers will find her much more interesting.

For each character try answering these questions:

- What is their gender? Do they identify as their birth gender?
- How old are they at the beginning of the story/series? How old are they at the end? Will they pass any major milestones, like starting school, puberty, etc.?
- What is their "sexual orientation"? Does this fall within what their society considers normal? If not, have they made their preference publicly known?

- Describe their build: skinny, thin, slender, wispy, athletic, solid, curvy, chunky, obese, stocky ... How does this compare to their peers? Are they average or an anomaly in some way?
- Eye colour. Do they have vision issues?
- Hair colour. Hair length and preferred style. Do they cut it within the time frame of the story or shortly before the beginning of the story? Are they growing it out? Is the length/style typical within their culture? Have they artificially changed the colour? What are their motives for changing it or bucking tradition? Does the colour or style have cultural significance?
- Do they have any tattoos? How many? What of? Where? What were their motives for getting the tattoos? Are they culturally significant or taboo? Do they have piercings? How many and where? What were their motives?
- Do they have any deformities or significant physical identifiers? Missing toes, fingers, or limbs: how did it happen? Misshapen ears, nose, lips, feet, hands ...how did it happen? Scars: how many and where? How did they get them? Limp? Weak arm or leg? Do they need a wheelchair?

Regarding #8: Please do your research. The way we talk and write about handicaps is changing. Someone in a wheelchair isn't necessarily looking for a way out of their chair. We need to write about diverse characters in a way that is compassionate, accurate, and respectful.

People who rely on wheelchairs, canes, seeing eye dogs, hearing aids, sign language, brail, etc. are not less. As writers we have a responsibility to make these characters whole, three-dimensional, fleshed out people who are not defined by their disability. We need to show them as capable, interesting, full of personality, and possessing their own strengths and weaknesses. Your main character may not be computer literate – that is their weakness. If the only weakness, or biggest weakness, of a character is that they are blind, rethink that character.

As you can see from this list, appearance is more than just a list of physical details. You need to consider why your characters choose the physical traits they have control over as well as the cultural norms they live within.

I'd like to pause here to talk about one of my biggest pet peeves: the character description data dump. Stop me if you've heard this one before:

My name is Kristy. I have straight brown shoulder length hair and just a few freckles on my cheeks and shoulders. I'm average height for sixteen but skinny. I'm pretty flat chested. I think I look pretty plain, especially without make-up, which my mother never lets me wear.

It's just as bad when a third person omnipresent narrator describes a character like this, or when one character describes another like this. First, it's overdone. Second, it's boring. Third, we don't think about ourselves, or others, in this way. The first time you meet someone you might notice what they're wearing or how unusually tall they are. The next time you might notice how they've styled their hair.

If it's someone you've known a long time you'd only really notice something about them if it's recently changed, like a hair cut or a new hair style, or a new dress.

If it's someone you might be sexually attracted to you'd notice a key feature – their figure, the way their clothes cling to their body, their hair or their eyes, their laugh.

When you're describing a character consider doing it in pieces. One person might comment on the colour of their eyes, another might note the colour and length of their hair, the character might complain about having to wear something that covers up their tattoos or having to take out a piercing for a formal occasion. By revealing these details gradually your story will feel more natural and you won't bog the story down with boring info dumps.

A Note to Male Writers: For the most part, women don't think about their boobs in any sensual or sexual way unless it's in a sensual or sexual setting – like deciding which bra to wear to accentuate their figure when getting ready for a date. Otherwise, we think about chaffing, how uncomfortable our bras are, the way the straps dig into our shoulders, the back pain from the weight of large breasts, how awkward they are when we run, etc. Also, when I meet another woman, I don't automatically gauge her boob size, or compare her to myself. Keep in mind, I'm a straight so I don't have a sexual attraction to boobs, but from what I've heard, even lesbians don't think about their own boobs in sexual terms.

Cultural Background

I'm Canadian, but my Grandmother is Dutch. I'm Catholic. My mom and her parents are Catholic. My dad's extended family is Mennonite, but not practising. The culture of my ancestors and extended family plays a role in shaping who I am and what I value.

In The Underground series, the Grieves family is Christian, the denomination isn't specified. They occasionally attend church and the twins do some activities with their youth group.

In the Rose Garden series, all five provinces worship Airon, the Sun God, but four of the provinces also have their own spirit guides: Earth, Metal, Animal, and Plant. Each province has its own culture, but people from one province often live in another creating a blend of cultures based on spirit guides, current province, and societal rank.

In my Zoedar series the royal family has a mixed bloodline, Human and Alaran. This changes the sorts of magical abilities they have.

- Where does the character's family come from? How many generations ago? How do the people around them view immigrants?
- Does your main character or anyone in their extended family speak two languages?

- Is your main character a mix of cultures or religions? Does this mix cause tensions in the household? Does this mix cause tensions in their society?
- If the character's parents, or the character and their spouse, have different faiths, how do they choose which to follow and which to raise their kids in?
- Are there unique traditions still being upheld? Feasts or festivals to celebrate? Special foods or drinks? Are these foods hard to find?
- Do the younger generations of the extended family embrace the "old" culture or reject it in favour of the culture they're now immersed in? How does the older generation feel about these opinions?

Family, culture, and religion are a complex web. You'll find yourself moving back and forth between them as new details in one area ripple into others.

Family

We don't grow up in a bubble. We have parents or some adult in a position of authority over us. We have siblings or other children around us. We have our own children, or nieces, nephews, and other young children to help teach or care for. We have extended family or communities or clans. Whatever shape your characters family will take will shape them in a variety or ways.

Families can take so many shapes, with a variety of step-parents, half-siblings, etc. I am using heteronormative pronouns in this list to keep it concise. Your families can have any combination of mothers and fathers that is suitable for your stories.

How you answer these questions will depend on the age of the character you're describing and their role within your story.

- Mother and father. What are their names? Are they married? Does the character know them? Does (did) the character live with them? Any step-parents? If they don't know their parents, who did they grow up with and why? Do they get along with their parents or caregivers? Are they alive?
- Do they have any siblings (full, step, half)? What are their names? List the birth order. Which ones do they get along with? Do they know them? Did they grow up together?

- Did the character grow up in a happy and stable home? If not, what sorts of problems did/do they encounter?
- Mother's/Father's Family: Grandparents, aunts, uncles, cousins. List anyone important to the character in some way. Why are they important?
- Have any important, or influential family members died? How does the character feel about these deaths? How recent was the death?
- Spouse, significant other, lover, etc. Do they have one? Do they have more than one? Have they had any in the past? Are they interested? Are they questioning their sexuality or exploring it in any way? Do they openly embrace an identity that we here on Earth at this present time consider "non-traditional"?
- Do they have any children? What are their genders, names, birth order, and ages? Who is the other parent? If not, why did they choose not to have children? Or was it a choice at all?

So often writers make the main character an only child. Or one or both of the main character's parents are only children so there are no aunts, uncles, or cousins. This makes it easier for the writer. No big messy Christmas dinners to write. No family trees to remember. No big list of names taped to the wall (I do this, it's useful).

In many cultures and regions, even in North America, this is not the norm. Perhaps your Main Character is an only child, or only has one child, but their parents likely had siblings as that was the norm until only a generation or two ago.

If you are writing anything in a fantasy or historical setting remember that before modern medicine a lot of people died of very mundane things. Families were big because you needed that many people to work a farm and because if you had ten kids only half of them would survive to adulthood. Not to mention the lack of birth control. The size of the families in your stories should fit your time period, culture, religion, access to medical aid, etc.

You may never include any of your main character's extended family in the book but having that family there in the back story changes them. An only child of two only children will have a very different experience of Christmas, or birthdays, then a child who has siblings and cousins, especially if they grow up close. It shapes your personality and preferences in a big way.

There's some research on birth order and the effects of large extended families, take a look at them or ask your friends for their experiences. Talk to your siblings. Their experiences growing up will be slightly different from your own memories.

If you're writing science fiction on the other hand, limited family size may be a part of your world building or plot – population control because of limited space, be it on a planet or a ship, is a common trope. Or perhaps only certain cultures are allowed certain numbers of children.

I've made a case for more children, more siblings, more cousins and aunts and uncles, but the truth is, not everyone wants children and not everyone can have children.

In historical fiction you're more likely to get large families because there was no birth control and a woman's desires to be childless would have been overridden by societal norms unless she was exceedingly wealthy and had enough siblings to satisfy society's marital demands on her family.

In urban fantasy, any fantasy with access to birth control, or science fiction, child-free women, and child free couples, can exist. And in our modern world they do exist.

People put their careers first. People choose not to pursue expensive fertility treatments. People choose not to adopt in the face of infertility. People simply don't want children, for no other reason.

Our culture is still one that puts undue pressure on women to have children. It's difficult for a childless woman to get her tubes tied, far more difficult for her than for a childless male. Writing stories about adults who don't have children, for a variety of reasons, will help ease that pressure, and the stigma around being childless. (We still call a childless married couple DINKs – Double Income No Kids).

What about when your character doesn't grow up with their own family, or with any family? They could be an orphan, growing up in an orphanage, with someone in the community, or an extended family member. They could be a ward of the state, or legally adopted. Maybe there was a plague, maybe you're in a post-apocalyptic wasteland, a very dangerous one, maybe your main character was kidnapped as an infant. Maybe your characters are growing up in a culture where babies are all raised in communal settings, so they know their nannies or teachers and not their parents.

You may have a culture that has boarding schools, or a separation of generations, or your young character is a run away, growing up on the streets. Sometimes biological family is replaced with gang leaders, older kids who stand as protectors or mentors, or authority figures within the establishment. These changes to the family structure will in turn change your characters maternal or paternal urges, their interpersonal interactions, and their views on certain aspects of their own, and other people's cultures.

Spouses and marriage is another big part of fiction, even in books that are not specifically romances. We have romantic sub-plots, or we have characters that are already married (parents of main characters for example, or background characters). But marriage doesn't have to be the Christian definition every time.

Hand-fasting, common-law, casual lovers, same-sex partners, polygamy and polyamory are all possibilities. As with any minority or marginalized group, respectful, accurate representation is key. A group marriage situation where everyone communicates and respects each other? Or two married couples who date amongst themselves? Or a couple who have an open marriage? Great! Better than falling back on the "jaded, jealous lovers" trope.

At the same time, we need more examples of loving, committed relationships of EVERY flavour in fiction. Yes, disagreements and misunderstandings build tension and tension sells the story. Yes, we needed stories of people walking away from abusive situations, and we still do, because we still have people in real abusive situations who need inspiring. But we need examples of what to strive for, of good solid marriages – not perfect marriages, just good, loving marriages, where people make-up, where people talk to each other and listen to each other, and where they actually get to grow old together.

Home – Past and Present

Home includes a few things like the country, state, and city/town in which they grew up and/or live. It's also the size and type of house they live(d) in, and the emotional conditions of their home(s).

You'll want to adapt these questions to the age of your character, their life stage and situation, and the genre of your story.

- Country, state/province and city/town – where were they born, where did they grow up, where do they live now?
- How big was the home they grew up in? Were they rich or poor? Was it crowded or roomy? Did they have their own room?
- How big is the home they live in now? Are they rich or poor? How many people live there? Do they have their own room?
- Was there any abuse in the home when they were children? If so, who was abusing whom, when, what sort of abuse, how/when did it end?
- Did everyone in the home get along? Were there tensions because of believes or opinions?
- When did they grow up? Was there a war going on? What were the popular songs and styles?

Religion/Beliefs

This is important no matter what genre you're writing, and whether you are using a religion that is practised on Earth or one that you have built for your story. Religion has always played a crucial role in societal and personal interactions, decisions, and opinions.

You already build the structure and tone of your religion in the culture stage. At this stage you're figuring out how your character identifies and interacts with their religion.

1. What is the dominant religion in the region your character lives in? Are there other religions practised in the community or nearby? Are their denominations or sects within the religion? If yes, which one does your character or their family follow?
2. How devote is your character? How devote is their family? Their community? How often do they pray or attend services? How deep or genuine is their belief?
3. Does your character agree with the social and political opinions of their religion? Where do they disagree? Are they vocal in their disagreement?
4. Does your character have knowledge of other religions that exist in your world? What does their religion say about other religions? Do they agree?

5. Did your character convert into their current religion? How long ago? Will they convert to a new religion during the story? What is their reason for doing so? Converts to a religion often act differently than those born into a religion.
6. Do they hold any special role within their religion? Are they a preacher, priest, prophet, etc.?

Even in science fiction religion is important. Often science fiction skims over religion completely, opting for a view of the future in which people are analytical and scientific and don't let religion get in the way anymore. Still, having a star ship officer who watches mass on holo-vid once a week, or who wears a traditional Sikh turban, or who needs the weekend off to attend the bar mitzvah of their son, adds cultural depth to the story and personal depth to the characters. Even Star Trek showed a Klingon wedding at one point.

Religion doesn't always have to equal fanatics, which is common in science fiction. The advanced, scientific, rational crew comes up against a population of die-hard, tech-fearing religious fanatics worshipping some hokey sounding deity in a cave or forest somewhere is a tired trope, and a potentially dangerous one. Religion on its own isn't evil and not every person who follows a religion is a fanatic. Lots of people have done horrible things in the name of religion, everything from excluding people or denying them rights and privileges, to genocide. Yes, your story can feature that type of fanatical organization, but maybe balance it out with rational, religious characters who don't fear technology or change.

Fiction gives us the chance to explore both the best and the worst of any situation, but all too often only the worst of religion is explored.

Job/Education

Depending on the age of the character, their economic standing, the time period of the story, and the formality of your education system, you're going to come up with very different profiles for this section.

For characters who are children or youth:
1. How long have they been in school? How long will they be in school? What do they study?
2. What subjects do they enjoy? What subjects do they excel in? (The answer needn't be the same to both these questions)
3. Do they focus on their education, or on the distractions like friends, romance, or out-of-class adventures?
4. How successful are they academically? How much emphasis does their family place on academic success?
5. What do they want to or plan to do when they finish school? Does their family approve of this choice? Do they agree with the plans their family has for them?
6. Is their school experience different from their siblings' or friends'? If so, how and why?
7. Do they attend a boarding school? Vocational or trade school? Are the schools segregated by gender

or culture? Does this affect their friendships or family relationships?

For adult characters:
1. How long have they been out of school? Or are they still attending a university or trade school or apprenticeship program? If so, how long will they be there?
2. What did they study? How long did they attend school? Were they successful academically?
3. What did they dream of doing with their life? What did they end up doing with their life?
4. Where do they work? How long have they worked there? Are they good at their job? Do they enjoy their job? Are they looking for a better job?
5. If they are not currently working is it by choice? Are they looking for work? How do they feel about their current unemployment?
6. Are they options for career advancement? If so, does your character want to advance?
7. How does your character balance work and personal life?
8. Is your character being faced with down-sizing? Layoffs? Other instabilities? (Farmers facing uncertain weather conditions? Or a drop-in demand for a crop?)
9. Is your character considering upgrading their skills? Going to re-employability training?

10. How far does your character have to travel to get to work? Does your character travel as part of work?
11. How many hours a day do they work? Which hours do they work? (late shift, split shift, day shift, casual, freelance, full-time)

In modern North American culture school and work takes up a large part of a person's day. In your fictional culture it may be similar, or it may take up less of their day, or be less stressful. Farmers have very different lifestyles from lawyers or engineers or teachers.

Preferences

For each item on this list, make a list of their favourites, the things they like versus the things they love, the things they're obsessed with, the things they hate with a passion, the things they just sort of avoid, or any allergies. Is their opinion in line with cultural norms? (If they're Irish, do they like whiskey? If they're Ukrainian, do they hate perogies? Are they into pumpkin spice everything?)

- Foods and Drinks
- Celebrities
- Animals/Pets
- Movies/Plays/Entertainment Sources
- Music
- Hobbies/Activities
- Colours
- Weather/Seasons
- Holidays/Feasts/Festivals
- Chores/Mundane Tasks
- Clothing/Style
- What they find attractive/annoying in prospective romantic partners

I don't drink coffee or tea. Or hot apple cider for that matter. I rarely drink pop and when I do I prefer clear drinks (ginger ale, lemon-lime), fruity ones, and root beer – I don't drink colas. I prefer milk or chocolate milk, and if I need a hot drink it's hot chocolate. Because most people have coffee, tea, and cola or ice-tea on hand I often have to bring my own drinks to parties or settle for water.

I mention this because it shows how your character's preferences can impact the story. I confuse a lot of people because I don't drink coffee or tea and it means I have to provide for myself in many situations.

Does your character love an animal they're allergic to? Do they love something that is culturally reserved for another group of people? (Girls who play with toy cars or boys who play with dolls, for example.) Do they hate something that is so culturally engrained as universally-loved (like coffee) that they startle people with their opinions? Do they have guilty pleasures? (I'll be honest – I actually like Nickelback).

Personality and Quirks

Name, appearance, and personality – those are the things people will remember about your character. While name and appearance are easiest to get out there, personality is the one that will really stick with the reader. It does take time to develop. As you go through the Preferences section and the Physical Attributes section, make note of your character's motives and secrets – those will be a useful part of their personality.

Here is a list of other things you can consider when crafting their personality:

- Describe their sense of humour: type (dry, boisterous, sarcastic, lewd), who it shows around, maybe they are different to different people. Is this a defense mechanism?
- What are they afraid of? The dark, clowns, spiders, etc. but also things like failure, or losing someone.
- How tidy/messy are they? Are they bothered by other people's messes?
- Opinion of the opposite/other gender(s)?
- Opinion on sex, sexuality, being sexually active, etc.
- How loud is their voice? When is it loud/quiet?
- Are they ever shy? Wary?
- Introvert/ambivert/extrovert? What is their personality type according to different tests?

- Are they leaders or followers? What do they want to be? What do they end up being?
- Pet peeves and bad habits? Guilty pleasures?
- How do they react to getting into trouble? To raised voices?
- When they are feeling strong emotions do they crave open spaces or small spaces? Do they want to be alone or with people? Which emotions inspire which reactions?

Take a look in the worksheet section at the back of this book for a full character interview that offers more insight into developing or discovering your character's personality.

Often, I find a character's personality will develop as I write them. They're offered a drink and it's only then I realize they hate coffee. I had one character in Rose Without Thorns turn out to be extremely snooty, but also a follower. His attitudes were copied from those of the people around him. When the power structure changes, so do his opinions because fitting in is more important to him than his own opinion. I didn't know this about him when I outlined the book.

When you make these discoveries add the details to your notes on the character.

Abilities/Disabilities/Talents

When you did the physical description of your character you may have included a physical disability or deformity, but there are also mental and emotional "disabilities" to consider. As well as things your character is naturally good at, or has extensively trained in.

As with physical disabilities, remember that, when it comes to conditions like Downes Syndrome and Autism, these people don't need to be cured. These conditions do affect their way of life, but they are people, capable of a full range of emotion and eager to experience life and the world, the same as anyone else.

On the reverse side, while everyone has something that they're sort of naturally good at, or have enough interest in to get better at, it's easy to overplay this and make your character a savant or whiz kid or prodigy. Most people aren't those things. They may have a good ear that helps them learn their musical hobby of choice more easily, but they aren't the next Beethoven or the next A-list rock star. Your character may have a good head for numbers and ace their high school math tests, but that doesn't mean they're going to be a Nobel Peace Prize winning mathematician or physicist.

- Does the character have any natural talents? How do they apply those talents to their career, education, or hobby? Does this make them more driven? Or do they slack off because "it comes easy"? Is it a talent their family or society sees as useful?

- Does the character have any mental health issues? This may include but is not limited to: PTSD, bipolar, anxiety, or depression. Have you done adequate research into the diagnosis and treatment of the issue you've chosen to write about?
- Does the character have any mental or physical developmental delays? Does the character have any genetic or chromosomal defects? This may include but is not limited to: FASD, ADHD, ADD, Downes Syndrome, Autism Spectrum, ODD, cerebral palsy, or MS. Have you done your research?
- Does your character have any supernatural or "mutant" abilities? Are these abilities inherent in their species or are they an anomaly? What are the capabilities and limitations of their ability? How or where do/can they practice or receive training?
- Does your character have any magical powers? Are these abilities inherent in their species or are they an anomaly? What are the capabilities and limitations of their magical powers? How or where do/can they practice or receive training?

In my writing I strive for honest, compassionate representation. I've written suicidal characters and I've written characters with PTSD due to sexual assault. In both cases I did my research and attempted to show a reality that was not glorified, sensationalized, or romanticized.

If I could ask one thing of you as you build your cultures and your characters it's this: please offer the people you are representing in your work, the people struggling with mental health issues, the minorities, the marginalized, with honesty, compassion, and respect. That doesn't mean rainbows and sunshine for everyone. It means do your research, get Beta readers, and take a little time to ask yourself if your writing is representing these people, or exploiting them.

Example 1: Angel of Light

The Angel of Light is an Alaran character from the early history of Zoedar. She appears as a historic reference in the novels and features in one short story in the Histories collection. Because she is so minor I don't have a lot of background information for her.

<u>First Name</u>: Arianna

<u>Last Name</u>: Never mentioned – not sure yet if Alarans use last names or not

<u>Titles</u>: Angel of Light

<u>Height and Build</u>: She is average height for an Alaran female, which is 6-8 inches taller than average for a Human female. She has a full but slender build and a soft face.

<u>Hair and Eyes</u>: Her hair is blonde with soft pink highlights; these highlights are natural. Her eyes are extremely light brown flecked with pink. She wears her hair long. As a younger woman she wore it up in elaborate twists as is the style of her people. During her pregnancy she wears it in simpler styles.

<u>Other Physical Attributes</u>: She has a large set of feathered wings. The feathers are mainly white. The feathers at the "elbow" joint and the pin feathers are pink.

<u>Species and Culture</u>: She is Alaran in species and culture. She embraces a more rural lifestyle, living in a simple home instead of one of the marble homes in the city.

Religion: She worships Sadeah, the goddess of law and order and offers respectful adoration to the rest of the pantheon.

Family: Her parents and possible siblings are never referenced. She has one lover whose identity she keeps secret. She has one son – Argrider.

Home: Her home country is the Alaran moon. She lives towards the edge of the city in a more rural area in a small cottage. Her childhood was pleasant.

Preferences and Personality: Favourite colour is pink, the colour of light. Her favourite season is summer. Her favourite holiday or feast is the summer solstice. She prefers simple dresses and hair styles. She enjoys music but doesn't play. She has no pets. She is peaceful and cheery and thou she comes across as demure she is quite strong-willed.

Abilities and Talents: She has the ability to manipulate the brightness of light in a space. She can radiate light.

If I were to lengthen her story, or feature her in more stories, I would use this character sketch as a starting point and add in family, home, and preference details as they became important to the story.

Example 2: The Five Rose Princesses

In the Rose Garden series there are five princesses. They all have red hair because of a magical pact that was made by their soul-ancestors (or previous reincarnations) with the chief spirit guide. Hair colour can be a big identifier, so I had to find other ways to distinguish between the girls.

First Names: I had considered giving them all "Rose" names like Rosalyn, Rosalie, Rosie, Roseanne ... but decided that it would be too confusing. They already looked a bit alike. Instead they ended up with the following names: Rheeya, Vonica, Betha, Taeya, and Ashlynn/Mallory.

Last Names: The upper class in this world are twice-named, meaning they have a double last name, separated with a hyphen, like "Black-Mountain" or "Golden-Heart". Commoners have a single last name like "Iron" or "Mason". The princesses all got Rose related last names that tied them to their province. Rheeya Stone-Rose, Vonica Bright-Rose, Betha Rose of Roses, Taeya Living-Rose, Ashlynn/Mallory Jewel-Rose. These last names serve to tie each princess to the province she rules.

Titles: When being introduced at a formal function or when signing a formal letter, their names and titles are as follows:

First Name Double-Last Name, # of Rebirths Princess of the Province, Protector of the Pact.

So Rheeya becomes: Rheeya Stone-Rose, 11th Princess of the Stone Clan, Protector of the Pact.

<u>Height and Build</u>: All five girls are within 6 inches of each other in height. Rheeya is solid, stocky. Vonica is slender but curvy. Betha is athletic and solid. Taeya is wispy. Mallory is full-figured but athletic.

<u>Hair and Eyes</u>: They all have auburn/red hair, but they wear it differently. Rheeya wears hers up at the beginning of her story but eventually switches to loose or pulled back from her face. Vonica almost always wears her hair in a way that hides her scars. Betha is forced by the fashion and tradition of her people to wear hers in elaborate twists and braids – she later cuts it. Taeya starts out with simple braids and moves to something more elaborate. And Mallory has the thickest hair of them all, so she wears hers in a single braid. Rheeya has grey eyes, Vonica's are a golden brown. Betha has light brown flecked with grey. Vonica's are a rich brown, and Mallory's are hazel.

Other Physical Attributes: Vonica has extensive scars on her cheek and neck from a childhood accident. She is the youngest and was always the awkward clumsy one. Vonica and Betha are more athletic and graceful. Aside from a few freckles there are no other distinguishing marks.

Cultural Background: Their culture is based largely on early Celtic Europe. There is a large wealth gap.

Family and Home: Mallory is the only one who knows her parents. The other four were raised by a nanny at the Temple Complex in the Province of the Sun. They grew up together, as sisters. They moved to their own provinces at twelve. They all feel quite lonely and have bonded with their personal servants and palace staff more than with other nobles.

Religion: They all worship Airon, the god of the sun, as well as their own spirit guides, the ones aligned with the province they rule.

Education: Extensive in history, theology, politics, diplomacy, and literacy. Basics in math.

Jobs: They hold court, listening to petitions as well as judging criminal cases. They have religious obligations. They supervise the guilds.

Preferences and Personality: Because there are five girls I won't do the full list, just the ones that are most important to their characters.

Rheeya: She likes her tea served from her favourite clay tea set and with a side of honey cakes. She has no pets. She likes joyful, simple music but has no musical talent. The colours of her people are earth tones and greys – she prefers warm browns. She hates rainy weather and cloth of silver dresses, and she finds the religious ceremonies tedious. She is warm and kind with a loud laugh. She dislikes cold traditions and ceremony.

Once she finds her strength she is solid, and unyielding, but fair.

Vonica: She loves books about adventure and travel. Her favourite place is the library. She has no pets. She's never taken a liking to music because she doesn't like to dance. The colours of her people are golds and reds. She hates being stared at because of a large scar from a childhood accident. She is soft-spoken but extremely smart and surprisingly daring.

Betha: She is loud, opinionated, and blunt. She hates to be penned in. She doesn't like anything, clothes, weather, spaces, events, that leave her feeling restricted or caged. She is forceful and demanding, often just doing things instead of waiting or taking the "proper" channels. She is loyal and values the loyalty of others. She is afraid to admit to people that she feels out of place in her own life.

Taeya: Like Betha she likes open spaces. She likes simple clothes and playing with her hair. She loves spring and fall. She is a fan of theatre and reads a lot. She surprises everyone because she's always been seen as quiet, as a bit of a follower, as she grew up in Betha's shadow, but she has a loud laugh and a sneaky sense of humour and she smiles easily. She is afraid of horses, even though she's supposed to like them and is the first princess in her province not to have a pet.

Mallory: Mallory likes pants and nice shoes and bright colours. She likes wine and beer and spicy foods, particularly an Indian curry. She grew up apart from the others in a very different culture and often feels lost, confused, frustrated, and very restricted. She's educated but not in the ways of "this world" so people view her as dumb or easily controlled. She is resilient. Though she is afraid of letting people down, the other princesses view her as a 'breath of fresh air'.

From World Building to Story Writing

The biggest challenge I have with world building is stopping. But you must stop, or at least set it aside, at some point, and start writing the story. As we see in our own world, cultures never cease to change and grow. They are complex, living, breathing things. Fictional cultures must be frozen in place while we write, providing a solid framework for the story, then, when the story is done, we can continue evolving our worlds in preparation for the next story.

Once you have your settings, your characters, and some idea of the plot you intend to write, whether you're a planner or a pantser, you're ready to write. Keep your notes close at hand and start writing.

Start as close to the inciting incident as possible. This means don't start with pages of scenic description. I'm sure your mountains are stunning, and your cities are architectural wonders, but the opening pages are not the place to go on in detail about them. In fact, you should avoid long rambling descriptions at all costs. Now, to be fair, "long" is a subjective term and will vary depending on the pacing of your work, and the genre you write.

I already mentioned that much of what you wrote in the world building stage won't appear directly in the books – so why bother with it? Because it influences so many things.

Your elf character will react differently to other elves than to humans if you've considered the racial tensions between them. You may never say "Elves are racist" but you will show it in the way your characters talk and act.

I don't like coffee. That wouldn't be a big deal in London in the pre-industrial era before coffee beans were imported to England, or even in the early days of coffee when people of my social standing wouldn't have had easy access to it. But now, in the middle of North America's caffeine and coffee culture, I'm an oddity. Knowing not only your characters' preferences but how the other characters will react to those preferences will colour many of their interactions.

That single mother looking for work, is there a stigma against her? If there is, it will be a lot harder for her to find work and she may face more sexual harassment in the process, if not, her experience will be very different.

In these cases, you won't outright say "this country has a stigma against unwed mothers" or "everyone loved coffee, it was the national beverage and was symbolically linked to success and over-achievers", but you will know these facts to be true and you will write characters who know these facts to be true.

The same goes for settings. You may never outright say "their architecture was based on the Ancient Romans of Earth" but you will have a mental picture of their city and will use words (like rows of fluted pillars in clean white marble) that evoke images of Rome or Greece or India or wherever you are drawing your inspiration from.

If "long" is a subjective term, how do you know if you have too much information? Too many details? Here are a few pointers:

1. If you're making lists, you're giving too much information. If you have to stop every time you enter a new space or meet a new person and list a whole bunch of descriptive things, you're giving too much information out at once.

2. If the details you're giving are not important to the development of the plot or character leave it out for now. Don't include it unless it's important to the moment or it's an important piece of foreshadowing.

3. If you give it to a Beta reader or editor and they say something like "it was good, but I found myself skimming past whole paragraphs" you've got too much description in too big of chunks.

Here's an example of #1 done wrong:
They walked into Mary's living room. The carpet was a neutral tan, but the yellow walls made the room

feel warm and welcoming. There were few pictures on the walls, mostly smiling faces that looked similar enough to each other to be family. The couches were brown, the kind you could sink into after a long day of work. There was a long coffee table the colour of dark chocolate and adorned with a vase of silk flowers.

Do you have any idea what's going on? Do you have any idea which of those details is important?

They walked into Mary's living room. The whole room was done up in tans and browns giving it a comfortable, homey feel.
"Oh, hey, neat photos," Mark said. He set his beer on the coffee table and went to take a closer look. "Relatives of yours?"
"Yeah."
"I could tell. This one has your chin."
"That's because that's me about twelve years ago."
"Huh, no kidding."
"Come and sit down," Mary said. "You said you wanted to talk." She settled on the couch and patted the cushion next to her.
"Yeah, sure."

We know a lot of the same details already, and you also know who came into the room, and that he wanted to talk to her about something. The scene is more dynamic and moves the story forward. It would be easy as the scene progresses to add details about the comfort of the couches and the flowers on the table, if they are even necessary. Sometimes less is more and it allows the readers to fill in the gaps, making the story more personal for them.

Which rolls right into #2. Maybe it's actually important that she has silk flowers on the table because she has an allergy that will be important to the plot. Maybe they were from her wedding bouquet and she's a young widow and she hasn't told this new lover about her past yet. If not, it wouldn't hurt to leave them out.

Does it matter how cushy the couches are? Unless you want to make some comment about their luxury, or their cheapness, as a comment on the character of their owner, or they will hinder the movement of a character at some crucial moment, is it really important?

And it may not be important now. Maybe Mark comments on how soft and saggy the cushions are and two chapters later Grandma gets stuck there just when there's some emergency that requires her to get up quickly. By revealing the detail about the couch earlier you'll be able to run the emergency scene much quicker, with more drama and tension.

If you're making mistakes with regard to points #1 and 2 your Beta readers and editor will likely pick it up. If you're not sure about the length of your descriptions, ask for opinions. "Hey, do you think the descriptions need to be condensed or spread out or something?" If you have honest, helpful readers they will tell you the truth and help you make your book better.

    Description can also help set the mood of a scene. You don't want to say, "the amusement park was creepy after dark" or "funerals are sad", there are no real emotions in those statements, they're too flat.

    Ben had been to the amusement park many times over the years, always on bright, sunny, summer days when the rides were up and running, their lights and music going, and the crowds of people laughing as they moved from ride to ride. This could have been a completely different place.
    The lights on the rides were off leaving only the streetlights over the sidewalks, their orange glow hazy in the spring mist. Odd shapes lingered in the mist, shadows that made Ben's throat tighten until he got close enough to make out a sign or a garbage can. And always expecting something to start up with that carnival organ music at any minute.
    His friends were laughing, seemingly unaffected by the shadows and the silence and the damp mist that clung to everything. One of them threw a beer can off into the shadows. It clattered, unseen in the dark. Ben half expected something to throw it back.

This is a little heavier on the description, but it is still interspersed with action. You can tell that Ben, and his friends, are moving through the space. This is important when you need to use large chunks of description. This physical motion through a setting, from the entrance of the park to wherever things are going to get weird, keeps the scene from feeling stalled or stagnant. As long as the characters or plot is moving forward there is action. Sections like this example are good as low action points, places where the reader can catch their breath between exciting scenes.

This scene builds a sense of something being wrong. You can feel Ben's heart pounding, feel the mist against your skin, and hear his friends' laughter echoing around you.

When you have to give larger chunks of description for whatever reason, to build mood, to explain something, or just to set up a scene, don't rely on sight alone. What can the characters smell? Or taste? Or hear? Or feel? Smell is so often overlooked in stories but it's powerful. I'm sure you can remember the smell of someone's hand cream, or cigars, or baking and those smells bring back wonderful memories. On the other hand, you probably remember the smell of a hospital waiting room, or garbage dump, or even a person's cologne – smells that may bring back less than pleasant memories. For PTSD sufferers and abuse survivors, smells can be a trigger.

Something else to keep in mind is that different people will notice different things when walking into a new space. A snooty character might notice if two pieces of furniture clash or if something looks cheap or tacky. They may also notice an expensive piece and show appreciation for it. The family-oriented character will notice the photos on the wall. The retail worker who's been on their feet all day will not notice much of anything until after they've dropped to the couch and put their feet up. What a character notices when they enter a new space or meet a new person says a lot about that space/person but also about the character doing the noticing. Take note, when you walk into a room, where are your eyes drawn to first?

World building is about more than just settings. It's about social interaction, history, economics, and more. Fortunately, most of that is easy to slip in as needed with quick side comments from the narrator or in dialogue.

"I thought you were third in line for the throne?"
"No, it's the crown prince, and then his cousin, the queen's nephew. I'm fourth."

We entered the temple and bowed to the priest on duty. Behind him a young man in a white tunic scraped wax off the marble floor.

"A new acolyte, I see," my father said.

The priest, an old friend of my father's, nodded. "The manual labour teaches them humility, so they will be better priests. By the time they become bishops they'll have forgotten it all again."

Ben counted the inventory six times but each time he came up four bags short. He reported the shortage to his boss who just shrugged. "I'll mention it to the guard. Thanks."

The guard wouldn't do anything about it, he knew. When things went missing it was likely on the orders of someone with more money or more power and the guards weren't going to stand up to that kind of power for a lowly shop keeper. No, best to just write it off as an expense of doing business.

Each of these examples tells you something about the world they occur in. The first is a specific piece of personal information, probably critical to the plot in some way. The second reveals a little about church hierarchy and about attitudes within the church. The third reveals a corrupt economic and political structure.

As each of these stories progresses more details can be revealed in similar ways. I call this layering. Apply the details and information in thin coats when needed until a complete story is formed. You will find this method keeps your story moving at a good pace, prevents the reader from skimming over long paragraphs, and gives your story a more natural feel.

Good storytelling is about entertaining your reader with interesting characters moving through interesting settings while grappling with an interesting plot, whether it is dark, or suspenseful, or romantic. That means adding realistic depth and detail without boring the reader. It means letting your characters be living, breathing, complex beings with likes and dislikes, opinions, hopes, fears, and goals. It means using descriptive language economically, so that every word counts as you build your settings. And it means plots and plot twists that respect the characters and their motivations and desires, story lines that uphold the suspension of disbelief in the reader.

My last piece of advice is this: nothing you write is set in stone – not in the story, not in the outline, not in the world building.

If something isn't working, change it. You may have to evaluate how those changes will ripple through your culture or story but making those changes as needed will strengthen your story.

Let the plot evolve as you get to know your characters. Let the characters evolve too. Keep notes, then go back and make notes on those notes so that when you go back to edit you can work towards consistent characters and plots.

If a character is evolving as part of the story show those changes so that when they make their decisions, it's believable.

When in doubt ask yourself: is this helping the story? If the answer is no, leave it out for now. If the answer is yes, leave it in. You can always come back later and edit it to be shorter or make better sense.

I find world building intensely interesting, so I found writing about world building refreshed me creatively and got me thinking about all my projects, got me excited for them again.

I've spoken with some authors for whom world building is a chore, a headache. If you're one of those authors, this book might help you keep everything in order. Or, I suggest, building pieces of your world as you need them and just noting things as you go along.

If you've never tried world building before this book is an excellent place to start. I also recommend reading extensively in the genre you plan to write, and world build in. Read with an eye for the culture, economics, politics, and religion of the characters in those books. Look at how climate changes architecture and culture. Look at how cultures treat their women, their poor, and their disabled. Read non-fiction as well and learn all you can about the variety of cultures that exist in our world.

If you're an avid world builder, you know it can be both exhilarating and overwhelming. It takes a lot of time and it feels like it will never be over. I hope this book helps you keep your ducks in a row and helps you turn your worlds into novels.

That's it. Now, go out and build yourself a world, a grand stage on which to perform your stories.

Good luck.

Bibliography

These are the books, shows, and movies I referenced in this guide. I do not own the copyright on any of them. I have also included references I use while writing, and recommended reading

Bishop, Anne. The Dark Jewels Trilogy. 1998-2000
Briggs, Patricia. Mercedes Thompson Series. 2006-2017
Bungie Studios. The Halo Universe. 2001-2017
Butcher, Jim. The Dresden Files. 2000-2015
Cameron, James. Avatar. 2009
DiMartino, Michael Dante; Konietzko, Bryan. Avatar: The Last Airbender. 2003-2008
DiMartino, Michael Dante; Konietzko, Bryan. Avatar: The Legend of Korra. 2012-2014
Eddings, David. The Belgariad. 1982-1984
Eddings, David. The Mallorean. 1987-1991
Geely, Holly. The Dragon's Tooth.
Hamilton, Laurel K. Nightseer. 1992
Jacques, Brian. Tales of Redwall. 1986-2011
Kripke, Eric. Supernatural. 2005-2018
Pierce, Tamora. The Immortals. 1992-1996
Pierce, Tamora. The Song of the Lioness. 1983-1989
Proust, Marcel. The Proust Questionaire. (English translation/summary available online: https://www.vanityfair.com/magazine/2000/01/proust-questionnaire)

Roddenberry, Gene. Star Trek: Deep Space Nine. 1993-1999

Rowling, JK. Harry Potter. 1997-2006

Sabrina the Teenage Witch. 1996-2003

Schreyer, Casia. World Building Worksheets, https://www.smashwords.com/books/view/794468

Tolkien, JRR. The Hobbit. 1937

Tolkien, JRR., Jackson, Peter (Director). The Lord of the Rings Trilogy. 1954-1955 (books), 2001-2003 (movies)

Uckleman, Dr. Sarah L., Dictionary of Medieval Names from European Sources: https://dmnes.wordpress.com/tag/nanowrimo/, https://dmnes.wordpress.com/2015/11/15/nanowrimo-balancing-truth-and-accessibility/, https://dmnes.wordpress.com/about-the-dmnes/.

Zelazny, Roger. Unicorn Variations, Unicorn Variations. 1983

Worksheets

I've included several worksheets to help with the outlining process and with various stages of the world building process as well as samples of these worksheets filled out for various projects.

Feel free to photocopy these worksheets, to type up your own versions, and to modify them to suit your needs. You are also welcome to use these worksheets, or variations thereof, with students in school or in workshops.

I have put together an 8.5x11 version of the worksheets and made it available as a free .pdf download. The link is available in the Bibliography.

Again, this .pdf is for personal, school, and workshop use, and they may be shared or modified but may not be sold.

Sample Character Profile - Physical

Full Name: Ethan Grieves
Nicknames: None
Age (range) during story: 14-15 years
Height: 5'2", average height, still growing
Weight/Build: Skinny
Eye Colour: Brown
Hair Colour/Length: Sandy copper, worn a little long
Gender/Sexuality: Male, heterosexual

Parents Names: John & Ina Grieves
Siblings: Shawna Grieves
Significant Other: Kyra (first crush)
Children: None in scope of story
Important Extended Family Members: None

Place of Birth: Complex 48
Date of Birth: Not said, 3rd generation underground
Race/Nationality: Father is Irish-American, Mother is German-American

Notable Attributes: some light freckles, very pale

Sample Character Profile – Extended

Name: Tomas Mason
Physical Strengths: Strong, lean, callused hands
Personality Strengths: Honest, loyal, dedicated
Physical Weaknesses:
Personality Weaknesses: Stubborn, common born

Likes and Favourites: Tomas enjoys a cold drink after a long day of work, he likes his cousin's son, and his father, he likes the satisfaction of a job well done. He's most comfortable in the mountains.
Dislikes and Least Favourites: Tomas hates dishonest, greedy people. He finds most nobles to be stuck-up and ignorant of what's important. He hates wet, rainy weather.

Exceptional Skills: Good at prospecting new places to mine, good at basic physical labour, a motivator
Magical Abilities: He is the princess's soul mate, otherwise, no magical abilities
Advanced Technical Abilities: N/A
Job: Miner, Stone Clan Prince

Sample Character Profile – Backstory

This is the form I use for Zoedar

Full Name & Titles: Meryum Reigh Hukaru
Birth Month: Summer Sol
Element: Fire-Kissed
Magic: Healing – Alaran based
Hair Colour: Auburn
Eye Colour: Caramel brown
Height: Just below average
Build: Slender, athletic
Parents: Tritaton and Catrana Hukaru
Siblings: Sepherym
Key Childhood Events/Backstory:
-at her birth her mother slipped into a coma for three years
-she was born a twin, a very rare occurrence in the Royal Family
-she was raised by Queenie Arbutus for three years
-just before her fifth birthday she was caught training with Troy and was put into training at five
-at eight she gets her own tower
Romantic Interests:
-Troy Arbutus – he respects her and loves her. He calms her fear that no man could love someone so unladylike
-Lars Veles – crown prince of Eastcourt. He is very interested in claiming and taming Mery by any means. She doesn't love him or trust him.

-Erjon Edain – lord's son in Tantaria and Mery's ally in the war.

-Suitors – very few are named. Most have their name on the list out of political interest rather than romantic interest.

Friends & Allies:

-Sepherym – though they are separated by the war they remain in contact and send aid to each other

-Christopher – one of her classmates, they train together, and he rides East with them at the start of the war

-Sir Zuan – Mery's squire master, becomes one of her advisors

-Sir Taggart – Troy's squire master, becomes one of Mery's advisors

-Lord Edain – Erjon's father, he helps Mery escape Eastcourt and provides his home to her as a base of operations

-Lord Veles – distant relative of both Jackson and the Edains, an ally of Meryum's during the war

-Andrake – became friends when he moves to Caprex. He makes her smile and keeps her temper in check when he can

Sample Species/Culture Physical Profile

Name: Humans (Chronicles of Zoedar)
What Others Call Them: Wingless Ones (Alaran insult)

Height Range: 4'6" – 6'10" with a few people falling outside that range on either side
Height/Build Difference Between Genders: Females tend to be shorter than the males
Eye Colours: Full range of what is normal for Terran Humans
Hair Colours: Full range of what is normal for Terran Humans with the addition of an Elemental Marker, a streak of hair near the front in some shade of one of seven colours.
Skin Tones: Caucasian and Mediterranean

Unique Physical Attributes: Elemental Marker, known as a Goddess Lock.
Geographical/Environmental Adaptations: N/A

Sample Species/Culture Details

Name: Giants
Tech Level: Stone/Early Metal Age
Political System: Tribal, Clans
Religious System: Spiritual, Medicine Men, no religious book, no church buildings, often carve totems of the deities
Deities: God of Toil (main deity), they also show respect to the other 8 deities

Social Structure:
Each tribe is led be a council of elders, this is not necessarily a hereditary position and can be held by men or women
Each tribe has a Medicine Man or Wise Woman
Almost no caste or class structure as they have a bartering economy

Marriage Customs: Two giants move in together. A large house warming celebration is held.
Legal System: Tribal council stands as court system
Education System: Apprenticeship based
Opinion of Other Cultures: Untrusting, prefer to be isolated, more because of their own introversion than any negative encounters.
Opinion on Genders/Sexualities: Genders are fairly equal with each Giant doing the job they are best suited

to, physically and personality wise. Females give birth but are not automatically the primary caregiver. No one bats an eye at transgender, non-binary, or homosexual individuals.

Magical Abilities: None

Opinions on Magic: Do not trust it or those who use it

Sample Setting Profile - Countries

Country/Region: Metalkin Territory
Climate and Weather: Similar in climate and weather to Eastern Canada or Northern Ireland. Damp, cold/cool in the winter, warm in the summer.
Terrain Details: Some low mountains and foothills in the southwest corner, lots of mines in the west and southwest. North and east boundaries are ocean coastline, very rocky. Central region is mostly farmland.
Plant Types & Amounts: Very little forest. Lots of grain farming. Lots of grass for grazing animals.
Wild Animals: Deer, packs of smaller wild dogs, rabbits, rodents, squirrels, birds
Domestic Animals: Sheep, goats, pigs, hawks, chickens

Architectural Style: Medieval Britain
Fashion Styles: Noble women wear a lot of jewelry and cloth of gold or cloth of silver. Style is medieval European.
Urban/Rural Differences: Only a few cities, mostly wealthy merchants, the guilds, and nobles. Paved roads, buildings with proper windows. In rural areas roads are unpaved, homes have no glass in the windows.
Population Density: Higher in urban areas

Sample Setting Profile – Cities/Towns

Name: Sun-Song Estate
Size: Single walled manor house with attached village of a hundred people or so.
Population Density: Low
Architectural Style: Medieval Europe village
Historic Period: Feudal
Overall Wealth: Moderately Wealthy
Districts: Manor house, manor courtyard and stables, village center, farms
Road Quality: Main road is cobble-paved, the rest are dirt or mud
Police/Law Enforcement: There are guards employed by the lord of the manor, the manor lord is the judge, anything he can't deal with goes to the capital to be dealt with by the princess.
Crime Rate: exceptionally low
Most Common Crimes: petty theft, drunken brawl
Dominant Culture: Sun Temple, Sun worshippers
Political Climate: Mostly stable, no radical sects
Regional Traditions: None of note
Overall Citizen Happiness/Prosperity: Relatively high
River/Coastal Access: None
Primary Industry: Farming (grain and animals)
Secondary Industry: Smith, teachers, artisans

Schools/Research: Basic primary school, tutor at the manor house, children with potential as scholars or teachers are taken to the capital for further schooling
Health/Cleanliness: Roads are muddy in bad weather, as are pastures. There are animals, mainly chickens, in town. No serious plagues or sicknesses. An average peasant farm village.

Sample Setting Profile – Individual Location

Purpose of Building/Setting: Castle, country capital
Owner: Zoedavian Royal Family
City/Country: Caprex (city surrounding castle), King's Holding (province), Zoedar (country)
Indoor/Outdoor Location: Indoor, with extensive grounds and underground passages
Type/Size of Building: Castle/Fortress, very large
Architectural Style: Germanic castle, with high walls, towers, and courtyards
Décor: Interior is stone walls decorated with tapestries and paintings. Furniture is mainly wooden, solid, heavy, in a variety of stains. Rugs in some rooms for warmth and comfort. There are statues and pottery on display. The hall has large pillars. The ballroom has a second-floor promenade along one side and large doors that let out onto the gardens. The grounds include a lake, stables and pasture, and training grounds. The underground passages are mainly storage rooms, indoor training facilities, and dorms for the squires, knights, and guards.
Who Lives/Works/Plays Here: The royal family lives here along with the boys training to be in the army, royal guards, serving staff, stable staff, and advisors. There are often visiting nobles staying in the guest wing. There is a fairy family living by the lake.

Strange Occurrences: With so many young boys living there, pranks are common, and many have led to rumours of hauntings.

People's Opinions of Location: Grand, considered highly defensible, a symbol of prosperity and unity

Character Profile - Physical

Full Name: _____
Nicknames: _____
Age (range) during story: _____
Height: _____
Weight/Build: _____
Eye Colour: _____
Hair Colour/Length: _____
Gender/Sexuality: _____

Parents Names: _____
Siblings: _____
Significant Other: _____
Children: _____
Important Extended Family Members: _____
_____
_____

Place of Birth: _____
Date of Birth: _____
Race/Nationality: _____

Notable Attributes: _____
_____

Character Profile – Extended

Name: _____

Physical Strengths: _____

Personality Strengths: _____

Physical Weaknesses: _____

Personality Weaknesses: _____

Likes and Favourites: _____
_____
_____

Dislikes and Least Favourites: _____
_____
_____

Exceptional Skills: _____
_____

Magical Abilities: _____
_____

Advanced Technical Abilities: _____
_____

Job: _____

Character Profile – Backstory

Full Name & Titles: _____
Birth Month: _____
Element: _____
Magic: _____
Hair Colour: _____
Eye Colour: _____
Height: _____
Build: _____
Parents: _____
Siblings: _____
Key Childhood Events/Backstory:
_____
_____
_____
_____

Romantic Interests:
_____
_____
_____
_____

Friends & Allies:
_____
_____
_____
_____

Character Interview Questions

Imagine you are sitting down somewhere (a television sound stage, recording a podcast over Skype, sitting in a study somewhere with your quill and ink) and are conversing with your character. Try writing the answers in first person, in the character's voice, to get to know them better.

Add questions that expand on the character's answers, ask them to clarify things. Omit questions that do not apply to your character or your world. Of change the setting – ask your character *if* they lived on Earth today, what would their answer be. Rephrase the questions so you're asking the character about friends or family members.

What is your full name?
Do you like your name?
Who named you? Any interesting stories about how your name was chosen?
What does your name mean?
Do you have any nicknames? Do you have any official titles?
Do you like your nicknames? Who calls you which name?
What culture/nationality/species do you belong to?
Where were you born?
What is your birthday?

How old are you?
What is your gender? Your sexual orientation?

What is your natural hair colour? Have you coloured it? What colour and why?
How do you wear your hair?
What do you like about your hair? What do you dislike?
What colour are your eyes?
Do you like your eyes?
What is most notable about your appearance? What do you think others notice first about you?
What do you like most about the way you look?
What do you hate about the way you look?
What would you change about your appearance?

Tell me about your parents. Add questions here about step-parents if applicable.
Tell me about your siblings. Do you get along? Which was your favourite?
Tell me your most embarrassing childhood memory.
Tell me your first childhood memory.
Tell me your favourite memory of your parents, of your siblings, of your extended family.
How often did you see your grandparents, or other extended family members? Why? Did you wish you could see them more? Or less?
Do/did you have pet(s)? What type? When? What was/were their name(s)? Tell me about them.

Tell me about your house. What does it look like? What does your room look like? Do you have to share your room? Do you like living there?
Tell me about your neighbourhood, your neighbours. How close do you live to your neighbours?

Are you physically active? Do you enjoy exercise or sports? Which ones or why not?
Do you dance? Play music? Sing?
What other hobbies do you have? Why do you enjoy them?
What do others think of your hobbies?

What is your favourite outfit? Why?
What styles do you wear? What social group do you feel you fit into?
Favourite accessories?
Do you get along with your peers?
Do you have many friends? Do you consider yourself popular?
Tell me about your best friend. When did you meet?
Have you ever been bullied? By whom? What did you do about it?
Have you ever bullied someone? Who? Why? Did you ever apologize or try to make it better?

Are you dating/courting someone? Tell me about them. Why do you like them?

Are you married? Tell me about your significant other(s)?
Does your family approve of your romantic choice?
Does your partner's family approve of you?
Do your friends approve? Why or why not?
Is the relationship abusive? Are there red flags that it might become abusive?
Have you ever been divorced?

Do you have any children?
How many? How old are they?
Who is the other parent?
Did you adopt? Are you fostering?
What do they look like? Who do they take after?
If you have no children, why? Do you plan to in the future? If not, why?

What job do you want to do when you grow up? Why?
What job do you currently have? Do you enjoy it? Is this a career or a temporary/stepping-stone job? If it's temporary, what job are you aiming for?
Are you good at your job?
Are you in school? What grade/level? How long until you're done school?
Do you/did you enjoy school? What is/was your favourite subject? Your least favourite?
Tell me about your favourite teacher? Your least favourite?

Do you have magical powers? Describe them to me.
How does your magic work? Did you have to study?
Do you like your powers?
What do you do with your powers?
Do any of your friends/family have powers? What are they like?
How common is it for people to have magic powers?
What do other people think of your magical powers?

Tell me ten things that are on your bucket list.
If you could go anywhere in the world, where would it be and why?
If you could meet anyone, alive or dead, who would it be and why?

Do you have a maid, butler, or other serving staff?
What jobs do they do for you?
What's your favourite/least favourite:
Book?
Television show? Movie?
Video game?
Play?
Song?
Musician?
Genre to read?
Style of music?
Colour?

Food?
Drink?
Celebrity?
Sport?
Person?
Animal?
Season?
Holiday? Holy day? Feast?
School subject?
Thing to do on a Saturday afternoon?
Place to go for summer vacation?

What social media sites do you use?
What do you share?
How many friends do you have online? Followers?
Have you been bullied online?
Have you bullied or trolled someone?
Have you ever sent or received nude photos online?

What are the best ways to cheer you up?
What are the best ways to calm you down?
What are the five most annoying things someone could do around/to you?
What is one thing that always makes you angry?
What is the most annoying sound?
What is the grossest thing you've ever felt?
What is the grossest thing you've ever eaten?

Do you believe in a god? If so, which one? Why that one?
Do you attend religious services? Perform religious rituals?
Do you enjoy your religious obligations? Which ones? Which ones bore you? Which ones make you feel uneasy?
Do you agree with your priests/preachers/holy leaders? What do you agree with them on? What do you disagree with them on?
Is there more than one religion in your city/country?
Is yours the dominant/majority religion?
Do you know anyone who follows a different religion?

How does your family get from place to place?
Do you know how to ride a horse? Or a similar animal?
What type of car do you/your parents drive?
Do you use public transportation? Why or why not?
Have you ever been in an airplane?
Have you ever been on a space ship?
Have you ever been on a boat? What type? For what reason?
What fuels the car/boat/plane/space ship?
Have you ever travelled outside your country?

Have you ever fired a gun? If so, why?
Have you ever used a sword?
Have you ever used other weapons?

Why did you have to use weapons? Have you ever killed someone?
Have you been hunting? Fishing? Do you enjoy it? Is it a sport? A hobby? A matter of survival?

Have you ever done anything illegal or against family or school rules? Were you caught?
If you were caught, what was your punishment?
If you weren't caught, did you ever admit to it? Who did you tell? Why?
Were you ever wrongly accused of something? Were you found guilty or innocent?
Have you been to prison?
Has anyone in your family been to prison?
Have any of your friends been to prison?
What was their crime? Are they guilty?

What are your political views?
Do you support your current government?
What government policies do you agree with? Which do you disagree with?
What political party do you support?
Are there political radicals in your country? Do you support or oppose their views? Do you support or oppose their methods?

Have you ever been targeted for being a minority or marginalized person?
Have you ever been the victim of slander?

Have you ever been the victim of a violent crime?
What happened to you? Was the person who hurt you
ever caught? What happened to them?
Has a member of your family ever been a victim? What
happened?

Species/Culture Physical Profile

Name: _____

What Others Call Them: _____

Height Range: _____

Height/Build Difference Between Genders: _____

_____

Eye Colours: _____

Hair Colours: _____

Skin Tones: _____

Unique Physical Attributes: _____

_____

Geographical/Environmental Adaptations: _____

_____

Species/Culture Details

Name: _____
Tech Level: _____
Political System: _____
Religious System: _____
Deities: _____

Social Structure:
_____
_____
_____
_____
_____
_____

Marriage Customs: _____
_____
Legal System: _____
Education System: _____
Opinion of Other Cultures: _____
_____
Opinion on Genders/Sexualities: _____
_____
Magical Abilities: _____
Opinions on Magic: _____

Setting Profile - Countries

Country/Region: _____

Climate and Weather: _____
_____
_____

Terrain Details: _____
_____

Plant Types & Amounts: _____
_____

Wild Animals: _____
_____

Domestic Animals: _____
_____

Architectural Style: _____
Fashion Styles: _____

Urban/Rural Differences: _____
Population Density: _____

Setting Profile – Cities/Towns

Name: _____
Size: _____
Population Density: _____
Architectural Style: _____
Historic Period: _____
Overall Wealth: _____
Districts: _____
Road Quality: _____
Police/Law Enforcement: _____

_____

Crime Rate: _____
Most Common Crimes: _____
Dominant Culture: _____
Political Climate: _____
Regional Traditions: _____

_____

Overall Citizen Happiness/Prosperity: _____

_____

River/Coastal Access: _____
Primary Industry: _____
Secondary Industry: _____
Schools/Research: _____

_____

Health/Cleanliness: _____

Setting Profile – Individual Location

Purpose of Building/Setting: _____

Owner: _____

City/Country: _____

Indoor/Outdoor Location: _____

Type/Size of Building: _____

Architectural Style: _____

Décor: _____

_____

Who Lives/Works/Plays Here: _____

_____

Strange Occurrences: _____

_____

People's Opinions of Location: _____

_____

About the Author

Casia Schreyer lives in Southeastern Manitoba with her husband, two children, and six rabbits. She has published over half a dozen books including The Rose Garden Series for young teens and adults and the Underground Series for Middle Grade readers.

When Casia is not writing she likes to spend her time knitting or spending time with her family.

About Schreyer Ink Publishing

In addition to novels and non-fiction, Schreyer Ink publishes high-quality collections of short stories. New release information and updates are listed on our website. If you like our books, please consider becoming our patron on Patreon. And please, if you found this book informative or helpful, consider leaving a review on Amazon or Goodreads.

www.schreyerinkpublishing.wordpress.com
www.patreon.com/schreyerink
www.facebook.com/schreyerinkpublishing
schreyer_ink_publishing@outlook.com

Interested in submitting a story?

Schreyer Ink will be publishing 6 anthologies in 2018, and each year following. We accept 8 stories per collection unless otherwise stated. Please visit our blog for information on themes and reading periods.

We look forward to hearing from you.

Also Available from Schreyer Ink

ROSE GARDEN SERIES (C. Schreyer)
Rose in the Dark
Rose From the Ash
Rose Without Thorns

UNDERGROUND NOVELS (C. Schreyer)
Complex 48
Separation
Reunion

NON-FICTION (C. Schreyer)
Mature and Responsible Adult – Sometimes
The Virtual Launch Book
World Building Worksheets

NELLY-BEAN … (C. Schreyer & A. Ganz)
And the Kid Eating Garbage Can Monster (Available in English, French)
And the Adventures of Nibbles

SHORT STORIES, POETRY, & INSPIRATIONAL (C. Schreyer)
Easter Mysteries (Digital only)
ReImagined

OTHER NOVELS
Nothing Everything Nothing (C. Schreyer)
Pieces (C. Schreyer)
Case Files of the Supernatural (K. Cockrill)
A Religion of Insomnia (A. Ganz)

ANTHOLOGIES (Various Authors)
Open Minds
Twilight Madhouse Volume 1
Twilight Madhouse Volume 2
Twilight Madhouse Volume 3
Hell's Talisman
Slave to the Axe Song

Coming Soon

Underground 4: Training

Shawna and Axel have left Complex 48 for Complex 1 to begin a special education program. There, Shawna is reunited with Ethan's friend, Kyra. But things are not what they seem, not at the school, and not among friends.

Underground 5: Rebels

Ethan has remained behind in Complex 48, waiting for word from Shawna. In the meantime, he is contacted by someone who not only believes his story but wants his help.

Schreyer Ink Anthologies
- Canadian Creatures: June 2018
- Children of the Sky: August 2018
- Twilight Madhouse Vol. 4: October 2018
- Future Sense: December 2018

www.ingramcontent.com/pod-product-compliance
Lightning Source LLC
Chambersburg PA
CBHW072043160426
43197CB00014B/2604